SUBURBAN COMMUNITIES

Program in Judaic Studies
Brown University
BROWN STUDIES ON
JEWS AND THEIR SOCIETIES
Edited by
Jacob Neusner
Wendell S. Dietrich, Ernest S. Frerichs,
Calvin Goldscheider, William Scott Green, Alan Zuckerman

Number 5
SUBURBAN COMMUNITIES
The Jewishness of American Reform Jews

by
Gerald L. Showstack

SUBURBAN COMMUNITIES
The Jewishness of American Reform Jews

Gerald L. Showstack

Scholars Press
Atlanta, Georgia

SUBURBAN COMMUNITIES
The Jewishness of American Reform Jews

© 1988
Brown University

BM
197
.S46
1988

Library of Congress Cataloging in Publication Data

Showstack, Gerald Lee.
   Suburban communities : the Jewishness of American Reform Jews /
Gerald L. Showstack.
      p.   cm. --(Brown studies on Jews and their societies ; no. 5)
   Revision of the author's thesis (Ph.D.)--Brandeis University,
1983, which had title: The Jewishness of Reform Jews.
      Bibliography: p.
      ISBN 1-55540-234-8 (alk. paper)
      I. Reform Judaism--United States.   2. Jews --United States-
-Attitudes.   I. Title. II. Series:
BM197.S46   1988
305.6'2296'073--dc19   88-10075

Printed in the United States of America
on acid-free paper

in memory of

Louis Showstack z"l

"As man discovers his I, his desire for perpetuity guides his range of vision beyond the span of his own life... he discovers the succession of generations...he envisions the line of fathers and mothers that had led up to him. He perceives then what commingling of individuals, what confluence of blood, has produced him, what round of begettings and births has called him forth. He senses in this immortality of the generations a community of blood, which he feels to be the antecedents of his I... And he therefore senses that he belongs...to the deeper – reaching community of those whose substance he shares... The people are now for him a community of men who were, are, and will be – a community of the dead, the living, and the yet unborn – who, together constitute a unity... The past of his people is his personal memory, the future of his people his personal task. The way of his people teaches him to understand himself..."

(Martin Buber, *On Judaism*)

Contents

List of Tables

Foreword

In the past, in America no less than in Europe, Jews tended to live in separate neighborhoods where the density of the Jewish population was high. Most were religiously observant, practicing the traditional rituals of Judaism and organizing their lives around their unique cycle of weekly and seasonal holy days and festivals. The segregation of places of residence and the observance of religious ritual implied as well the segregation of jobs, schools, and institutions, along with social pressures toward cultural conformity from family and neighbors and limited social contacts with non-Jews. Residential segregation and traditional Judaism were linked to each other and resulted in high levels of Jewish communal cohesion, powerful social and economic networks, and social control. Jews interacted primarily with other Jews, shared their daily lives and annual cycles within the Jewish community, and, in the process, separated themselves, as they had been separated by the larger society, into we and they; in-group and out-group; Jews and non-Jews. The continuity of the Jewish community through the generational transmission of Jewish values and culture was thereby assured.

Much has changed over the last century as the lives of Jews have been transformed. Residential patterns are not restricted by others and voluntary segregation in closed neighborhoods does not characterize most American Jews. People move away from family and friends, into new statuses and new places. These new social and geographic locations do not necessarily have high levels of Jewish density. Thus, only in the modern period is it meaningful to ask: What happens to the Jewishness of the community when neighborhoods are no longer primarily Jewish and when communities are no longer defined geographically?

Along with these sociodemographic changes, the religion of the Jews changed dramatically during the last century. Clearly the Judaism of American Jews in the 1980s is not what it was in the past, either in Europe or in America. The most conspicuous changes have been in the decline of religious ritual observances, decreasing attendance at synagogue services, and the switch in denominational affiliation away from the orthodox. No less important was the decrease in the centrality of Judaism in the lives of Jews. In the context of secularization, we pose the central analytic question, Does the decline in religiosity imply the decline of the Jewish community or do new forms of Jewish expression emerge to redefine Jewishness in the transformed society?

From the point of view of those who are traditional (or orthodox), the reformation of Judaism represents a threat to the power and authority of the established rabbis and the traditional community of faith. Reform and change in Judaism are thus treated as part of the assimilation process. From this point of view, the switch to Reform Judaism is treated as the beginning of the decline of Jewish community and total assimilation. The orthodox predicted that as Jews became less observant and adopted religious reforms, it would be but a short step to limited Jewish education; ignorance of Jewish history, language and culture; intermarriage with non-Jews; and structural and cultural changes. Total assimilation was only a matter of time. For the traditional Jewish community, being a Reform Jew symbolized the last of the Jewish dominos before the end of Jewry in the next generation.

So it often seems to traditional Jews toward the end of the 20th century in the United States. Jews who live in neighborhoods with high levels of Jewish residential density, who adhere to orthodox restrictions on travel and work on the Sabbath, who continue to lead their lives according to a special calendar that is Jewish, and restrict contact with non-Jews to formal, business relations view Reform Jews who do not share this lifestyle as assimilated and lost to the future of the Jewish community in America.

The ideological conclusions of traditionally observant Jews need to be raised as empirical challenges to social science research and not treated as the inevitable consequences of socio-cultural changes. We need to ask, How Jewish are Reform Jews? What holds them together as a Jewish community? How do Jews maintain a community when there are low levels of Jewish density in their neighborhoods and their lives are surrounded by non-Jewish culture and American, not Jewish, life styles? These are the critical analytic questions to be researched systematically in order to understand the processes of change and continuity among American Jews.

In this volume, Dr. Gerry Showstack confronts these issues with the depths and skills of a trained observer of the Jewish community and the tools and methodologies of social science. He systematically and carefully unfolds the depths of Jewishness among Jews who are neither orthodox in religious practice nor resident in dense Jewish urban neighborhoods. With detailed data and mature insight, he documents what makes Reform Jews Jewish in America and the importance of their community. He shows the connections between the social and residential patterns of Jews, on the one hand, and how they feel about their Judaism and their Jewishness, on the other.

On the surface, this volume reports on an in-depth study of the memberships of two Reform Temples in one metropolitan area, at one point in time. It describes and analyzes the relationships between Jewish density and the attitudes and values of Reform Jews and interprets these relationships in quantitative and qualitative modes of analysis. But this is more than another focused and limited empirical research project. The theoretical and substantive conclusions from this study have broader applications to the analysis of change and continuity among American Jews and to theories and research on the acculturation and assimilation of American ethnic groups.

Showstack combines two sociological theoretical traditions in his analysis of Jewish identity. First, he incorporates the valuable lessons from the Chicago school of urban ecology and its updated revisions, emphasizing the structural conditions of neighborhood and the importance of local ethnic communities. Then, he turns to theories of assimilation and cultural pluralism, with its social-psychological orientation to attitudes, perceptions, and identification. Drawing on these and related perspectives, he goes beyond them to develop his own framework to study relationships between Jewish density (in geographic and associational dimensions) and the multiple expressions of Jewishness.

Focusing in detail on suburban Reform Jews, Showstack documents how their socioeconomic and residential background influences their Jewish density and, in turn, how current levels of Jewish density are linked to their Jewishness. These Jews are clearly not traditional in their religious observances and are removed from densely settled urban Jewish neighborhoods. As second and third generation Jews, they are distant as well from their immigrant roots, are relatively affluent and well educated, and are thoroughly acculturated Americans. Yet these Jews clearly identify themselves as Jews, have connections to others in the

Jewish community, behave in ways that identify themselves as Jews, and express Jewish attitudes and values. They constitute a community based on social interaction and life style, on networks and contacts, on shared culture and Jewish commitments. While their Jewishness is less based on traditional indicators of religiosity and Jewish residential density, their new forms of Jewish expression can hardly be described as trends toward total assimilation.

Presenting bivariate and multivariate statistical analyses, Showstack convincingly shows how these new bases of Jewishness emerge in complex ways. He documents the positive association of past Jewish density with current levels of Jewish density, even controlling statistically for the effects of educational level which is negatively associated with current Jewish density. In turn, he presents evidence to show how current Jewish density is positively associated with a wide array of measures of the Jewishness of these Jews, including how they identify themselves, their relations to non-Jews, perceptions of anti-Semitism, the role of Israel, Jewish educational experiences, and the importance of Jewishness in their lives and for their children. He posits a sequential pattern of associations, from background to current Jewish density to Jewish identification, while being fully aware that the causal patterns can only be fully investigated with longitudinal research designs.

From the statistical analysis and from his own in-depth interviewing and extensive observations, Showstack constructs four composite ideal types or profiles of American Reform Jews. These profiles translate the sophisticated and complex quantitative results into real and concrete illustrations of the diverse lifestyles of suburban Reform Jews, their background, their current Jewishness, and their aspirations for the Jewishness of the next generation. His insights and interpretations are drawn as well from his thorough immersion into the nuances of Jewish communal life and culture and a rare sensitivity to the American Jewish historical context. These multiple strategies of investigation and interpretation are anchored in a careful synthesis of previous research on the sociology of American Jews and their communities and, no less importantly, of the broader literature on American ethnicity.

Showstack concludes that Jews have by and large chosen neither to abandon their identity as Jews or relinquish their associational Jewish networks. He demonstrates that continued residential and associational concentration are of critical importance for strong Jewish communities, even in suburban settings and among less traditionally religious Jews. Thus, while ethnic networks exist in groups that are geographically dispersed, ethnicity is strongest among members who are geographically clustered. Along with social scientists who have focused on other ethnic groups in America, he concludes that ethnic clustering is not only a consequence of high levels of ethnic density but is also an antecedent of future ethnic clustering.

This book documents what Jewishness means in America, as Judaism is reinterpreted and as Jewish communities are transformed. Those who see only decline and weakness in the social, religious, and residential changes American Jews have experienced should examine the results of Dr. Showstack's study of *Suburban Communities: The Jewishness of American Reform Jews.* They will learn much to challenge their conclusions and assumptions. Others, who are concerned about improving the quality of American Jewish life and developing policies and programs to enhance Jewish continuity in America, will find important directions for constructive developments in this analysis. Indeed, we have before us a significant contribution to the understanding of the cultural and structural bases of emergent Jewish ethnicity in the 1980s.

Calvin Goldscheider
Program in Judaic Studies
Department of Sociology
Brown University

January 1988

Preface

The present monograph is a revised version of research originally prepared as a doctoral dissertation for Brandeis University. It represents an attempt to capture the multidimensional interplay of cultural and structural factors in the Jewishness of one segment of contemporary American Jews. Free to blend into the open setting of the American suburb, they choose rather to affirm their Jewishness and create Jewish community. Free to become simply Americans, they choose to maintain their identity as American Jews. This study is an effort to present an in-depth examination of their multiple identifications and adequately to portray the nuances and interrelations of their complex lives as American Jews.

I wish to thank Marshall Sklare of Brandeis University for his thoughtful guidance throughout the research and writing of the original study. My thanks go also to Egon Bittner, Gordon Fellman, and Bernard Reisman, also of Brandeis, for their efforts in reviewing earlier versions of this research. I am especially indebted to Calvin Goldscheider of Brown University whose criticism and insight were instrumental in shaping the direction of the study and whose confidence inspired the revisions and publication of this volume.

Given the contribution of these five men to my academic training, the views expressed here are perhaps not solely my own. The research and conclusions, however, are, as is of course final responsibility for them.

Sree Sudha Yerneni did a great deal of conscientious work in formatting the manuscript for publication. Her efforts are much appreciated.

Finally, I wish to gratefully acknowledge the several bodies who supported my research in its various stages. These include the National Foundation for Jewish Culture and the Memorial Foundation for Jewish Culture during the original research, and Brandeis University and the Program in Judaic Studies at Brown University during the process of revision and publication.

Gerald L. Showstack
November 1987
Kislev 5748

CHAPTER ONE

ISSUES AND PERSPECTIVES IN THE STUDY OF AMERICAN JEWISH ETHNICITY

I. The Issues and the People

Serious study of American Jewry in the 1980's is likely to lead to a case of schizophrenia. On the one hand, we are witness to the continuation and even the institutionalization of many positive signs of Jewish identification and cultural awakening begun in the late 1960's and '70's. Havurot exist both outside of and within established congregations. Jewish studies programs on campuses are an accepted part of the academic scene. Young Jews rally to the needs of other diaspora Jewries under seige.

We are told by popular authors that American society has never been more open to Jews and by social scientists that firm structural bases exist for the maintenance of the Jewish group in America.[1] Undoubtedly, these optimistic readings of the state of American Jewry have support in the American reality. A decade ago, a Jew was elected chairman of the board of Dupont; in 1987, a Jew is elected president of Princeton University. Though moving beyond traditional occupational roles and moving out of old Jewish neighborhoods, Jews continue to concentrate both residentially and occupationally and provide themselves with important bases for the increased intensive interaction so necessary for group cohesion.

And yet, at the same time, we are witness to dramatic changes in the Jewish family, changes resulting from increased divorce rates, extended periods of "singlehood," and the like, which leaves less than one in three American Jewish households consisting of two parents and children.[2] While we are told that intermarriage does not necessarily lead to quantitative losses for American Jewry, we cannot but look with concern at a situation in which intermarriage is becoming "normal" as virtually every American Jewish extended family has non-Jews within its ranks. The religious divisiveness so characteristic of Israeli Jewish society has begun to infect American Jewish society as well.

Which view of American Jewry is true? Who is right? The fact is that the American Jewish glass is neither half empty nor half full. It is both, half empty *and* half full at the very same time. Given this complexity of the American Jewish situation, one key to understanding is to examine communities in depth, rather than being seduced into either blanket optimism or pessimism.

The present study is an attempt to do precisely that. Its focus is on the ways in which the grouping of Jews in residential communities and friendship networks is related to attitudes on issues central to the continuation of the Jewish group.

The people studied are clearly identified as Jews. They are not the most marginal *in* or *to* the American Jewish community. And yet in certain critical respects, they represent the current margins and perhaps some future trends as well. They are Reform Jews, the "least traditional" of the American Jewish denominations. They are suburban Jews, far removed from the old urban Jewish neighborhoods. They are among the educational and occupational elite of American society. They ostensibly and perhaps even in reality are free at last to become simply "Americans," with no hyphen attached. Yet they have chosen to do otherwise. In the American suburb, they have chosen to establish Jewish community.

Understanding these Jews engaged in such "strange" behavior presents a fascinating and potentially revealing quest.

II. Perspectives in the Literature

Let us first put this study of American Jews in the context of past explorations of Jews and other American ethnic groups.

Several approaches may be distinguished in the sociological literature on the ethnicity of European immigrants to the United States and their descendants. These differences revolve around issues of the origin and maintenance of distinctive ethnic group identity and processes of adjustment and adaptation. Each approach implies a particular theoretical framework for the study of these ethnic groups in terms of both research foci and lines of analysis. A review of the literature reveals three basic types.

The first is exemplified in the work of Park, Wirth, and other members of the Chicago "environmentalist" school. As the name implies, the emphasis here is on the effects of the new host environment on the immigrants and their progeny. The focus is not, however, on the origin or maintenance of ethnicity in the new setting. Rather, the immigrants are seen as arriving with a full-blown religious and cultural heritage transported from the country of origin and with a concomitant sense of identity as a group. The stress is on those cultural and structural features of the American environment which serve to diminish and lead to the dissolution of ethnic distinctiveness.

The eventual absorption of these ethnic groups into American society, entailing of course their disappearance as distinct entities, is taken as a given. Normative issues as to the desirability of assimilation do not arise, as the latter is perceived as both inevitable and right. The concerns of this approach are more pragmatic: descriptions of the nature and content of the immigrant culture rooted in the European experience, and particularly a statement of the inexorable movement towards amalgamation into the host society.

The exodus from ethnically homogeneous areas of first settlement – the ghetto – is stressed, while continued ethnic clustering in areas of second and third settlement is treated as a form of residual behavior. The implicit direction of adaptation is towards the adoption of and eventual conformity with the white Anglo-Saxon Protestant model. Factors opposing this absorptive process, be they prejudice and discrimination by the majority or retreat by minority-group members into the security of transplanted microcosms of their Old World environments, are seen at most as temporary aberrations and delays in the predetermined assimilation process.

Louis Wirth's pioneering work on Jews in America, *The Ghetto*,[3] is a case in point. While the primary focus of this review of Wirth's study is criticism of his position, his study, first published in 1928, was a major early contribution to the sociology of American Jewry.

Wirth's study, however, has several significant flaws. While the population he is studying is comprised of east European Jewish immigrants living in Chicago's Jewish ghetto, the first half of his study consists of a description of ghetto life in *western* Europe. As east European Jews were not ghetto dwellers in the west European sense,[4] the first half of Wirth's study is virtually irrelevant for the second half of his book.

The main objection to Wirth's book, however, focuses on his assumption that the assimilation of Jews in America is inevitable. Colored perhaps by his own biography,[5] Wirth believed that once the American ghetto dissolved or at least once the Jews moved out of the ghetto, they would be shaped exclusively by the American setting and cease to constitute a recognizable ethno-religious group.

This view is based on Wirth's acceptance of the Chicago school's position regarding the primacy of the environment as a force shaping its inhabitants. Assimilation is seen as a progressive force and as a necessary prerequisite of democracy.[6]

The problems presented by Wirth's framework for analysis are manifold, even if we forego the advantages accruing from hindsight which informs us that the Jews have of course not disappeared within the general American population. Wirth posits that a minority group living in a society with a dominant culture different from its own will inevitably pass through a series of relationships between itself and the dominant culture: isolation, competition, conflict, accommodation, and assimilation.

The first weakness of this theory is that it does not specify a time period within which this progression of relationships is to take place. For this reason, there is no possible way of testing its validity. If a group will "inevitably assimilate," but only at some unspecified time in the future, the failure of any group to do so may be explained away by recourse to the position that while its members have not yet assimilated, they eventually will.

Another criticism of Wirth's scheme is that it does not specify the factors which generate movement from one stage of the process to another. As Etzioni states in his critique of Wirth and of the Chicago school position:

It is clear that under some conditions this process does not take place, while under some others it does. What are these conditions? Park and Wirth seem to have no systematic hypothesis on this point. ...what are the conditions under which the processes of assimilation are triggered or blocked? Park and his disciples introduce ad hoc factors which delay the 'natural' process... But these factors are not an integral part of the conceptual scheme.[7]

Ironically, though disregarding their implications, Wirth himself had pointed to some of the mechanisms which may facilitate ethnic group maintenance. As noted by Etzioni:

...one can find in Wirth's material some important clues on the nature of these mechanisms. One of the most important seems to be the common tradition reinforced by communication... There is common identity, tradition, values, and consciousness. Often there are common sentiments and interests based on past experience, education, and communication. The common bond is reinforced through ethnic newspapers, organizations, clubs, and synagogues, where members meet, even though they do not live next to each other and are not concentrated in one ecological area.

Jews and some other ethnic groups in America seem to pass from ecological, traditional, immigrant, 'totalistic' groups...to non-ecological, non-totalistic, modern groups...maintained by communication and activated in limited social situations and core institutions.[8]

Analysis of this combination of cultural and structural forces which reinforce ethnic group maintenance can in fact serve as a framework for research on Jews in America.

The second approach to the treatment of the immigrant-ethnic group phenomenon and of the dynamics of interaction with the host society can be succinctly subsumed under the two rubrics of melting pot and cultural pluralism. There are in fact significant differences between these two types and each has given rise to its own series of variants. Nonetheless, it is the similarities and common assumptions of these two positions which are of greatest interest to the present statement.

Here once again the various immigrant groups are seen as having arrived with religious and cultural baggage more or less intact. Emphasis is on the fusion in the American setting of imported local or regional identities into broader categories of national or religious identity. The particular village or city of origin of Italian immigrants is overlooked and even northern and southern Italians are lumped together simply as "Italians." Similarly, the specific place of origin of immigrant Jews is disregarded and regional identities that were salient among the immigrants themselves become irrelevant in the American setting. Galician, Lithuanian, and Polish Jews are identified simply as Jews, and even distinctions between earlier German Jewish immigrants and later east European arrivals lose much of their meaning.

A further focus in the melting pot-cultural pluralism approach is on the selective accommodation of aspects of the transported heritage as a consequence of interaction with the demands and norms of the host society and culture. While the ethnic (or religio-ethnic) groups are technically seen as creations of the American experience, stress is laid on their being constituted from imported material forged in the new environment.

Let us once again refer to the issue of residential concentration as a touchstone. The approach of the environmentalist school took such structural factors centrally into account, though disregarding evidence contrary to the outcome predicted. Both the melting pot and the cultural pluralism approaches, however, tend to treat structural features such as residential concentration as second-order considerations in their emphasis on the dynamics of cultural interaction between the ethnic group and the host society.

While structural processes were an essential focus of the Chicago school analysts, the primary interest of the melting pot and cultural pluralism theorists is the cultural dimension. Structural implications are seen by them more as normative and inevitable by-products. Though the general outcome foreseen by both adherents of the Chicago school and by melting pot theorists is similar, it is this different emphasis in the analysis of the process of assimilation which distinguishes between them.

The melting pot analysts focus research on contributions of the ethnic group to the emergent American culture and on the disappearance of the distinctive ethnic group culture with the adoption of the new American cultural alloy. For the environmentalist school, we remember, the direction of adaptation was towards the adoption of the quintessentially American white Anglo-Saxon Protestant model. The melting pot allows more latitude in regard to the final cultural product.

Structural integration of the various constituent groups in American society, though not a primary focus of the melting pot theorists, is taken in the melting pot scheme not only as a foregone conclusion, but as a "patriotic" duty. Integration is not only described as an inevitable outcome of the "melting" process, as what *will* be; it is presented as a desideratum, as what *should* be. It is assumed that widespread intermarriage will take place. The end of ethnic residential concentration is also seen as inevitable, in part as a by-product of exogamy. This assumed linkage between exogamy and residential integration, is, however, far from a necessary conclusion.

Cultural pluralism, while perhaps allowing for residential concentration, is not at all centrally concerned with it. Its focus is rather on the retention of distinct cultural features in the private sphere and on the concurrent adoption of uniform American norms and behaviors in the public sphere.

Advocates of cultural pluralism clearly felt that it was incumbent upon the members of each group to adopt those uniform cultural practices necessary for the efficient coexistence of ethnic groups living in the same society. All groups, for example, were to learn and use English as the common language of communication in the public arena.[9] Particular cultural distinctiveness was seen as properly reserved for the private sphere and as consisting primarily of those elements of the intrinsic culture of the group such as "its religious beliefs and practices, its ethical values, its musical tastes, folk recreational patterns, literature, historical language and sense of a common past..."[10] This dualism was seen as facilitating the functioning of the general society.

Some of the variants deriving from the melting pot-cultural pluralism complex take selected structural considerations more explicitly into account. In *Protestant, Catholic, Jew*,[11] Will Herberg traces the development of the ethnic group through three generations. He sees the answer to the gnawing question "Who am I?" provided for the first generation, no longer able to identify according to their village of origin, by groupings according to mother-tongue.

Reinforced by their also being defined by others according to these same foreign-language groupings, the former residents of distinct and various villages and locales within each country of origin come to identify as members of a broader ethnic group. The ethnic church comes into being and assumes a central role, as religious identification is perceived as the legitimate means of maintaining distinctiveness in the American setting.

The second generation, according to Herberg, was perpetually caught in the conflict of being neither exclusively members of their group of origin nor yet fully American. Some choose to assert their ethnic identity and become leaders within their own particular group. Others try, most unsuccessfully, to rid themselves of their particular ethnic identity. Most live continually with the tension inherent in being suspended between their two identities.

For the third generation, the native-born children of native-born parents, American identity finally comes as a natural birthright. They, however, says Herberg, have difficulty taking their ethnic identity seriously, and therefore seek recourse in their particular religious group identity as the context of identification and social location.

Given this identification according to religious group and given subsequent evidence of ethnically exogamous but religiously endogamous marriage, Herberg amends the melting pot into the triple melting pot of Protestant, Catholic, and Jew. His analysis, originating in nearly exclusive emphasis on cultural transformations, thus proceeds to a consideration of modifications effected through structural forces, and finally returns to a primarily cultural focus within his tripartite division of American society.

Herberg's scheme also falls short of providing a comprehensive analytic framework. His position both gives insufficient consideration to cultural aspects of ethnicity aside from the religious and virtually ignores structural supports of ethnicity except for endogamy. In his recurrent emphasis on the religious dimension, he overlooks additional components of ethnic identity.

In addition, though initially recognizing that for Jews alone the religious community is coterminous with the old ethnic group, Herberg in a later essay criticizes the synagogue as no longer constituting a "community of believers."[12] In doing so he misses the point of the continued broader ethnic function served by American Jewish religious institutions. Given his limited focus on Americanized versions of the religion of ethnic groups, Herberg would be equally surprised by manifestations of both more nationalistic and more traditionally religious components of ethnic identity. He would, for example, be hard pressed to explain both the strength and nature of American Jewish attachment to Israel and the return to Orthodoxy on the part of some young American Jews.

Structural considerations figure more prominently in the work of Milton Gordon. In *Assimilation in American Life*, Gordon identifies seven distinct components of the assimilation process.[13] He correctly allows for acculturation without structural assimilation. However, in predicting an assimilatory deluge following upon the heels of structural assimilation, he too overlooks significant possibilities for the continued maintenance of ethnicity.

Gordon overlooks the possibility of cultural continuities within the ethnic community that may persist beyond the stage of initial acculturation. American Jews dress, speak, work, pursue leisure-time activities, and even eat to a large extent in ways very much like other Americans. Nonetheless, within this general American lifestyle, points of cultural distinctiveness remain.

Gordon likewise overlooks structural supports of ethnic distinctiveness that may persist beyond what he defines as structural assimilation. For example, though Jews live among, associate with, and work at the same occupations as many other segments of the American population, non-random residential distribution, maintenance of largely Jewish friendship networks, and a skewed occupational distribution continue to serve as structural supports of Jewish ethnicity in America.

Thus beyond a significant degree of both acculturation and structural assimilation, there remain both cultural and structural supports for the persistence of the Jewish ethnic tie in America. Gordon's analytic framework, like Herberg's, provides an insufficient context for an understanding of American Jewish ethnicity.

The third approach to the study of American ethnic groups of European ancestry lays stress on the American locus of ethnogenesis[14] with primary emphasis on social structural variables and only passing reference to common cultural background. Thus Yancey, Ericksen and Juliani treat ethnicity as dependent on the structural factors of occupational and residential distribution and "dependence on common institutions and services...which reinforce the maintenance of kinship and friendship networks." Rather than viewing ethnicity as "an ascribed content" as in the cultural pluralism model or as a "temporarily persistent variable" as in the melting pot model, ethnic groups are seen as "emergent phenomena...produced by structural conditions" which are part and parcel of modern urban America.[15]

Yancey, Ericksen, and Juliani begin their article with a statement of the insufficiency of both the "assimilationist and pluralist perspectives":

> Both positions have emphasized the cultural origins of ethnic groups. This underlying assumption has never been tested, nor has the structural context of the argument been specified...
> Much that has been written about race, ethnicity, social class and community has centered around the issue of the importance of culture in determining life styles. Our review of this literature suggests that much of it is based on empirically untested assumptions about the importance of the portable heritage which a group brings from one generation and place to another.[16]

Their preferred focus is rather on the experience of the ethnic group in interaction with the structural features of the host society:

> We suggest that a more parsimonious explanation of ethnic
> and community behavior will be found in the relationship of
> the ethnic community to the larger macroscopic structure of
> the society...[17]

Their examination of this relationship deals primarily with the effects
on ethnic residential concentration of the occupational configuration of
American society during both the nineteenth and early twentieth cen-
turies and in modern urban America. They distinguish between the
relative dispersal of the "early" immigrants, who arrived before the cen-
tralization of urban employment, and the concentration of the later great
waves of immigrants from eastern and southern Europe:

> Before the concentration of large scale employment, work op-
> portunities for immigrants were scattered and their residen-
> tial locations were correspondingly scattered. In the latter
> period, to the extent that work opportunities were concen-
> trated, the immigrant "ghettos" were also concentrated.[18]

In the contemporary setting, Yancey, Ericksen, and Juliani discuss three
forms of the residential arrangement of ethnic groups: suburban "quasi
communities," black and Puerto Rican ghettos of relatively recent origin,
and residual urban villages.[19] In each case in both the historical and
contemporary analyses, they deal with the implications of residential
concentration or dispersal for the ethnicity of the group involved.

While stressing an important hitherto underemphasized dimension of
the study of ethnic groups, the nearly exclusive structural emphasis of
Yancey, Ericksen, and Juliani has two basic shortcomings in terms of
its suitability as an analytic framework for the study of contemporary
American Jewish ethnicity. The first is that the cultural dimension is
treated only as a consequence of structural forces. Over time, the cultural
dimension may in fact come to shape the structural characteristics of
the post-immigrant generations, for example through influencing both
occupational and residential choices.

Secondly, while recognizing the importance of such structural features
as interstices and new opportunities in the occupational structure of the

host society at the time of large-scale Jewish immigration to the United States, the Jewish experience is somewhat different from that of other groups. In their places of origin, Jews already lived not as members of the national or religious majority, but rather as members of a minority ethnic group. While it is important not to overestimate the transportability of ethnic cultural baggage, neither must we underestimate both the cultural and structural implications of having arrived with prior experience in establishing and maintaining ethnic community.

This experience stands in sharp contrast to that of other groups suddenly confronted with the jarring dislocation involved in the transition from "superordinate indigenous group" to "subordinate migrants."[20] While it is critical to recognize that Jewish ethnicity continues to evolve and change in the contemporary American setting, it is no less critical in the study of American Jews to adequately take into account their cultural and community-based structural heritage.

Thus while effecting a needed balance to the previous cultural emphasis, the theoretical position advanced by Yancey, Ericksen, and Juliani cannot in itself provide an adequate analytic framework for our present research interests.

Additional light may be shed on the recent shift to structural emphases from the observation that, in addition to the various theoretical perspectives outlined above for the study of ethnicity, there has of late been a great deal written *about* ethnicity. This writing focuses specifically on its "resurgence" and newfound legitimacy. What is in fact resurgent is not the phenomenon of ethnicity itself, but rather the recognition of the persistence and strength of the ethnic tie.[21]

It is precisely this recognition that may underlie the recent search for structural explanations in the theoretical literature. Analysis of the ethnic phenomenon primarily in terms of culture led to substantially incorrect hypotheses about its demise. Therefore, as the realization grew that ethnicity is still a powerful force in American society, recourse was sought in "hard" societal processes capable of sustaining the ethnic tie in the face of massive acculturation, i.e., in structural features of American society.

Among the writings on the ethnic "resurgence" are analyses which highlight the attempt by various groups to secure equal access for their individual members to the rewards of American society.[22] The social disruptions of the 1960's can thus be understood in part as efforts by specific groups, maintained by features of the American social structure such as residential and occupational concentration, acting on dissatisfaction with their place in that structure.

In this light, the shift to structural explanations in the 1970's is certainly a necessary corrective to the disproportionate emphasis on cultural factors which had dominated thinking on ethnic groups in American society. Despite widespread acculturation, structural factors in large measure sustained these groups. The most articulate examination of this dynamic in relation to American Jews can be found in the recent work of Calvin Goldscheider, most particularly in his reexamination of data from the demographic studies of the Boston Jewish community.[23]

III. The Present Research

A. Theoretical Underpinnings

The appropriate theoretical underpinning for an examination of aspects of American Jewish ethnicity incorporates elements of both the melting pot-cultural pluralism and structuralist approaches to the study of ethnicity.

Social structural features are critically important in the emergence and persistence of ethnic identity and community. The shift to structural explanations should not, however, obscure the continued role of cultural antecedents and consequences of these structural features. Recently, the ethnic activity of the past twenty years has in fact given rise to increased cultural awareness and demands – the search for roots, the demand for ethnic studies programs in universities. More generally, we must not lose sight of the potential impact of cultural background characteristics on social-structural configurations. Neither should we overlook the interaction of the latter with cultural factors such as attitudes, perceptions, and identification.

If, for example, residential concentration serves as one of the structural bases for the emergence and persistence of the ethnic group, what are the cultural background characteristics which, in addition to other structural considerations, motivate such non-random residential distribution? What are the cultural correlates and indeed the cultural consequences of this social-structural feature? What cultural factors in part underlie and are in turn affected by the associational networks which various structural configurations serve to reinforce? While the structuralists do not deny the existence of such cultural supports and implications, neither do they enumerate or examine them.

While ethnogenesis with its concomitant structural focus is especially appropriate in describing the emergence of groups formed totally in the United States, the combination of both structural and cultural foci is more necessary in dealing with American ethnic groups whose perceived common origin is more directly European. In the specific case of American Jews, the cultural focus becomes even more critical.

The ethnicity of Jews differs from that of other American ethnic groups such as the Italians, Poles, or Irish. While American Jews shared with these other ethnic groups a sense of local village or regional identity, Jews also already had in Europe a minority group culture and identity which they brought with them to the United States.[24]

East European Jewish immigrants to America brought with them and at least selectively succeeded in transmitting to their descendants the sense of being part of a distinct group and the desire to survive as such. They had lived among, but not as members of European national groups and considered themselves the chosen people,[25] regardless of the transformations and permutations later exacted upon this concept in the American egalitarian setting.

Also transferred to America, though certainly transformed in the process, was a sense of how to maintain such group distinctiveness and what were the necessary, if not sufficient, conditions to do so, namely Jewish communal culture and structure including its organizational and institutional expressions.

Therefore, together with sufficient attention to the impact of structural factors, the cultural component must also figure prominently in an understanding of the emergence and persistence of the Jewish group in America. Particular attention must be paid to the interaction of the cultural dimension with the structural supports of Jewish ethnicity.

B. Analytic Framework

Jewish density is the pivotal structural concept in this study. It is demonstrated to be a critical structural support of ethnicity. Jewish density is operationally defined by two variables: the proportion of Jews in the community in which the respondent lives and the proportion of Jews among the friends of the respondent. While the former measure is geographic or spatial and the latter is not, they are considered jointly as it is their combined effect which best conveys a sense of the social density of American Jews.

American Jews do not live in exclusively Jewish residential settings, except for specific attempts along these lines by certain ultra-Orthodox groups that constitute a distinct minority of the American Jewish population. There is no parallel in the American setting to areas of European cities which were first cleared of other residents and then designated as Jewish ghettos.

Exclusively or nearly homogeneous Jewish friendship networks, however, may serve as modern surrogates for homogeneous Jewish residential settings in providing high Jewish social density despite spatial mixing. Friendship networks that are primarily Jewish have also come to serve as potential surrogates for the intensive interaction within the extended family that formerly characterized Jewish social patterns.[26]

While American Jews do live in significantly varying degrees of Jewish residential concentration, analysis of residential concentration alone would result in a severely incomplete picture. The social density of American Jews is most fully reflected by examination of both residential and associational concentration patterns.

Measures of both residential and associational concentration are based on the perception of the respondent as reported in a questionnaire.[27] As the central concern is with the relation of these Jewish density vari-

16

ables to various other perceptions and attitudes of the respondent and to the respondent's identification with the Jewish group, the respondent's *perception* of residential concentration and friendship patterns is treated here rather than objective measures of these same variables.

Residential concentration and friendship patterns were selected from among variables which function as structural supports of ethnicity for reasons which have their source in both the general and the Jewish literature. From the general literature we note, in addition to those references cited in the previous sections, that these two dimensions are intimately related to the potential functions of the ethnic group. As Guest and Weed remark:

> Ethnic communities may continue to serve two principal functions... several decades after the great waves of immigration ended. First, ethnic groups may serve as political interest groups... A second function of ethnic groups is suggested by Louis Wirth's theory (1938) in "Urbanism as a Way of Life." Metropolitan areas – owing to their size, density, and heterogeneity – are often potentially, if not always actually, alienating and anomic. The organization of *associational and residential ties on the basis of ethnicity* may counterbalance some of the less agreeable aspects of urban life.[28] (emphasis added)

In terms of the specifically Jewish context, these variables are recommended by the particular attention they have received in previous research on the Jewish group in America. On friendship patterns, we note "The Friendship Ties of the Lakeville Jew" in Sklare and Greenblum's *Jewish Identity on the Suburban Frontier* and Herbert J. Gans' "The Origins of a Jewish Community in the Suburbs."[29] The special importance attributed by Sklare to Jewish friendship patterns is evident in his elevation of "associational Jewishness" – a residual form of Jewish identity based primarily on maintenance of mostly or exclusively Jewish friendship networks – to an independent status among types or modes of Jewish identification.[30]

The focus on residential concentration in the Jewish context has been twofold. Early research posited the central and critical function of residential concentration in maintaining the Jewish group, and as we have seen, went so far as to predict the disappearance of the latter subsequent to the end of the former. The other focus has been on the Orthodox or observant segments of the Jewish group and has dealt primarily with the necessity of Jewish residential concentration for the establishment and support of institutions and services necessary for the maintenance of their way of life.

The interest of the present research is in examining both the antecedents and consequences of Jewish density in relation to a suburban Reform Jewish population.[31] Jewish density functions in this analytic scheme alternately as both a dependent variable in relation to selected measures of social characteristics and Jewish background and as an independent variable in relation to selected measures of attitudes, perceptions, and identification.

It must be emphasized, however, that although the analysis is approached and executed in terms of this independent-dependent variable format for purposes of analytic clarity, we are dealing with correlational and not causal relationships. While it is clear that Jewish background precedes current Jewish density, the time sequence involved in the relationships between density, some social characteristics, and attitudes is simply not specifiable within the context of the present cross-sectional study. Further, we must remember the possible effects of potential intervening variables which are not included in this analysis.

Two additional relationships round out this analytic scheme. Background in terms of both social characteristics and Jewish background [32] may be related to the attitudes, perceptions, and measures of identification with which we are dealing, either directly or mediated through its effects on the Jewish density variables. The attitudes, perceptions, and identification of the respondent potentially also function as independent variables affecting Jewish residential and associational concentration.[33]

The analytic scheme upon which the present research is based may thus be succinctly summarized in diagram form:

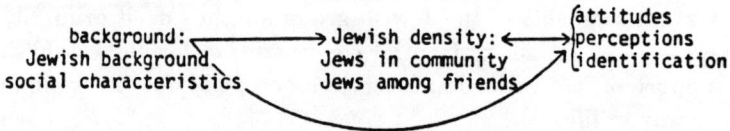

```
                                                    ┌attitudes
        background: ──────────→ Jewish density: ←──→│perceptions
     Jewish background          Jews in community  ↗ └identification
     social characteristics     Jews among friends
```

The main objective in what follows will be to analyze and interpret the various associations among these three sets of components. Primary emphasis is placed on the implied sequence of the effects of background on density and of density on attitudes, though also recognizing, as mentioned, that background may affect attitudes directly or indirectly and that attitudes may in fact affect density.

C. Research Questions

Johnston and Yoels suggest that "Ethnicity is a cultural tradition the behavioral and attitudinal import of which may be said to vary under given structural conditions."[34] They posit, following the classificatory scheme of types of residential community of Yancey, Ericksen, and Juliani that ethnicity is "strongest in the ghetto and decline(s) as we move toward the quasi communities of suburban America."[35]

It is surely the suburban setting that is already, and is becoming ever more so, that most typical for American Jews.[36] Study of ethnicity in the suburban setting certainly allows for full consideration of the complex interplay of structural and cultural features of the group in interaction with those of the American setting. While perhaps weaker in these suburban "quasi communities," however, ethnicity does not cease to exist or function there. Rather, the question becomes whether the nature and strength of ethnicity vary in relation to differences in the specific structural conditions which obtain in various suburban communities. Yancey, Ericksen and Juliani suggest that it does:

> It is possible...for ethnic networks to exist in geographically dispersed groups, yet the effect of ethnicity may be strongest among members who are geographically clustered... People

are more or less dependent on their community at various
stages in the life cycle... (Such) needs may be served by
neighbors, friends, or institutions. When these are of the
same ethnicity, the likelihood of ethnic behavior and identification with ethnic origins should be greater.[37]

Differences in ethnic background among members of the same group must
also be taken into account. As Yancey, Ericksen, and Juliani further
suggest:

The monolithic treatment of ethnicity, used in much contemporary empirical research, has not paid attention to differences within an ethnic group ...we suggest that it is not only
necessary to test for differences between groups, but to also
identify those conditions which produce ethnicity and ethnically related behavior.[38]

Given the importance of residential and associational concentration, one
would thus want to examine the potential impact of having grown up in
situations of different levels of residential clustering and with different
degrees of ethnically homogeneous friendship networks.

What then are the central questions to be examined regarding the ethnicity of Jews living in contemporary suburban America?

First, is Jewishness still a factor in critical behavioral decisions among
well-educated, affluent, acculturated American Jews living in an open
society? For such a population, who experience very few restrictions on
their residential and friendship choices, is the Jewish dimension brought
to bear on questions of where and among whom they choose to live and
with whom they choose to associate?

Second, for such a population, are differences in residential and friendship patterns associated with different attitudes in matters that relate
centrally to Jewish ethnicity? If so, which aspects of such attitudinal
sets are most strongly associated with such residential and associational
patterns?

Third, are differences in Jewish background related to differences in Jewish attitudes? Is Jewish background associated with differences later in life among highly educated, affluent, acculturated Jews in terms of attitudes along dimensions that relate centrally to Jewish ethnicity?

The questions raised and addressed in the process of this research are of course not limited to Jews. When members of an ethnic group are no longer restricted to living in segregated communities which by virtue of their concentration, limited size, and frequent interaction among their inhabitants are capable of exercising social control over their members, does that ethnicity remain a salient factor in the life of members of the group? We will address this issue as it pertains to, and in a framework adequate for its examination among Jews in the contemporary suburban American setting.

Notes

1. See, for example, Charles E. Silberman, *A Certain People*, New York: Summit Books, 1985 and Calvin Goldscheider, *Jewish Continuity and Change*, Bloomington, Indiana: Indiana University Press, 1986.

2. Sylvia Barack Fishman, "The Changing American Jewish Family in the 80's," soon to appear in *Contemporary Jewry*.

3. Louis Wirth, *The Ghetto*, Chicago: University of Chicago Press, 1928.

4. Jews in western Europe were often concentrated in designated areas within major cities, areas that had been cleared of their non-Jewish population specifically for this purpose. More typical of the situation in eastern Europe was that Jewish settlement was restricted to outlying geographical regions and Jews excluded from the major cities except by special permission. Within the areas open to Jewish settlement, Jews often lived in towns or villages. Thus the famous "shtetl" in the Russian "pale of settlement."

5. Wirth, of German Jewish parentage, was himself intermarried and remained on the periphery of American Jewish life.

6. Wirth's position is evident in the following statement made several years after the publication of *The Ghetto*: "Since consensus conditions and is the product of the participation of persons in a common life, the limits of consensus are marked by the range of effective communication. Consensus may disintegrate because communication between the individuals and groups who are expected to act collectively is reduced to a minimum. As John Dewey has pointed out, 'Everything which bars freedom and fullness of communication sets up barriers which divide human beings into sets and cliques, into antagonistic sects and factions, and the democratic way of life is undermined.'" (Louis Wirth, "Ideological Aspects of Social Disorganization," *American Sociological Review*, 5 (1940): 479) Wirth is thus in principle against that which divides people and thereby threatens "the democratic way of life."

7. Amitai Etzioni, "The Ghetto - A Reevaluation," *Social Forces*, 37 (1959): 258.

8. Ibid.

9. Recent support of bilingual education in the public schools is a marked departure from the classical cultural pluralism position.

10. Milton Gordon, *Assimilation in American Life*, New York: Oxford University Press, 1964, p. 79.

11. Will Herberg, *Protestant, Catholic, Jew*, Garden City, New York: Doubleday and Company, Inc., Anchor Books, 1960.

12. Will Herberg, "The Postwar Revival of the Synagogue," *Commentary*, 9 (1950): 315-325.

13. Milton Gordon, op. cit., pp. 60-83.

14. Ethnogenesis is a term used to highlight the emergence of ethnic groups -- such as the white southern ethnic groups in Chicago referred to by Yancey, Ericksen and Juliani – in the American setting, as opposed to seeing their formation in Europe (or elsewhere) prior to migration to the United States. It is usually associated with emphasis on structural factors as primary forces in the genesis of the ethnic group. See William L. Yancey, Eugene P. Ericksen, and Richard N. Juliani, "Emergent Ethnicity: A Review and Reformulation," *American Sociological Review*, 41 (1978): 391-402.

15. Yancey, Ericksen, and Juliani, op. cit., p. 392.

16. Ibid., pp. 391, 399.

17. Ibid., p. 399.

18. Ibid., p. 395.

19. Boston's North End is an example of an area classified as a "residual urban village." It became well-known as such as the subject of Herbert J. Gans' *The Urban Villagers* (New York: Free Press, 1965).

20. Yancey, Ericksen, and Juliani, op. cit., p. 392.

21. Among the more perceptive writings on the dynamics of the ethnic "resurgence" see the final essays in John Higham's *Send These To Me* (New York: Athenaeum, 1975). Analysis of the origins of the resurgent ethnic awareness among American Jews has focused primarily on the twin effects of: 1) the example set by black Americans in asserting their own group pride and 2) the psychological consequences of the Six Day War and the threat which immediately preceded it, deepened by its coming precisely at the time when American Jews were being excluded from the ranks and removed from among the leadership of the civil rights struggle.

22. See, for example, Daniel J. Elazar, *Community and Polity*, Philadelphia: The Jewish Publication Society of America, 1976, p. 23.

23. Calvin Goldscheider, *Jewish Continuity and Change*, op. cit.

24. It is the process of the transference of this minority group culture and its communal institutional manifestations and of the adaptation of both in interaction with the American environment which Sklare so amply describes and analyzes. See Marshall Sklare, *America's Jews*, New York: Random House, 1971.

25. The notion of "chosenness" looms large in the historical self-conception of the Jewish people, who saw themselves as chosen by God from the among the nations of the world. It is reflected in the traditional liturgy in the phrase "asher bachar banu" – "Who chose us" – and forms the basis of rabbinic stories elaborating on the selection process which led God to choose the Jews. Queasiness as to the particularistic nature of and implications of superiority associated with this concept has led in the modern period to its being confined to in-group discussion, redefined, or totally rejected among various segments of the Jewish group.

26. *Havurot*, Jewish quasi-communes and fellowships which arose primarily in the 1970's and were located both outside of and within existing congregational structures, are an interesting example of the institutionalization of associational networks functioning Jewishly (and perhaps more broadly as well) as surrogates for the extended family. See Bernard Reisman, *The Chavurah, A Contemporary Jewish Experience*, New York: Union of American Hebrew Congregations, 1977.

27. Details on the nature and execution of the survey may be found in Appendix A.

28. Avery M. Guest and James A. Weed, "Ethnic Residential Segregation: Patterns of Change," *American Journal of Sociology*, 81 (1976): 1109. Literature comparing the social dynamics of urban to those of suburban life has shown that many such social patterns hold across these spatial lines and are not specific to either city or suburb. See, for example, Barry Schwartz, ed., *The Changing Face of the Suburbs*, Chicago: University of Chicago Press, 1976.

29. Marshall Sklare and Joseph Greenblum, *Jewish Identity on the Suburban Frontier*, New York: Basic Books, 1967, pp. 269-290; Herbert J. Gans, "The Origins of a Jewish Community in the Suburbs" in Marshall Sklare, ed., *The Jewish Community in America*, New York: Behrman House, 1974, pp. 19-41.

30. The classification is taken from lectures by Marshall Sklare on "American Jewish Life and Institutions."

31. The criteria for selecting the population are discussed in the next chapter.

32. Jewish background is operationally defined as consisting of three components: 1) background Jewish density (proportion of Jews in community and among friends while the respondent was growing up); 2) aspects of the Jewishness of the respondent's parental home; and 3) Jewish education.

33. In addition, of course, there may be interaction effects among the measures of attitude, perception, and identification and between Jewish residential concentration and friendship patterns.

34. Barry V. Johnston and William C. Yoels, "On Linking Cultural and Structural Models of Ethnicity: A Synthesis of Schooler and Yancey, Ericksen, and Juliani," *American Journal of Sociology* 83 (1977): 734.

35. Ibid.

36. See Sidney Goldstein, "Jews in the United States: Perspectives from Demography" in Joseph B. Gittler, ed., *Jewish Life in the United States: Perspectives from the Social Sciences*, New York: New York University Press, 1981, p. 65.

37. Yancey, Ericksen, and Juliani, op. cit., p. 400.

38. Ibid., p. 392.

CHAPTER TWO

THE COMMUNITIES AND THE SAMPLE

I. Choice of Research Site

Having chosen to study suburban Jewish communities which differ in terms of their respective Jewish density, are there further guidelines in the literature on ethnicity which suggest additional defining characteristics for a subject population?

Among the factors stressed by Yancey, Ericksen, and Juliani in discussing structural supports of ethnicity is "dependence on common institutions and services...which reinforce the maintenance of kinship and friendship networks."[1] This emphasis suggests that a community identified by the affiliation of its members with some "common institution" might well serve as an appropriate population for community-based research on ethnicity.

The persistence of Jewish ethnicity in America cannot be attributed to immutable differentiating factors such as race. Religion, however, was the distinguishing characteristic which immigrants were not supposed to abandon as they were their language and so much else, but rather were supposed to adapt and maintain. Accepted until recently as *the* legitimate basis of distinction, religion serves functionally as a differentiating factor for Jews as the only major non-Christian group in the traditional American formulation of Protestant, Catholic, Jew. Religion is certainly a major cultural component of Jewish ethnicity and, through the institution of the synagogue or temple, a major structural element as well.

The function of religious institutions as the focus of ethnic community is documented by Herberg and by Greeley.[2] It is of course basic to Sklare's treatment of the "ethnic church" in *Conservative Judaism*.[3] Ellman in "The Ethnic Awakening in the United States and Its Influence on Jews" states that in the United States "churches and synagogues became the strongest bastions of ethnic culture."[4] Thus the synagogue or temple would serve well as an institution around which to locate the communities to be studied.[5]

26

If the current research would be conducted on communities of suburban Jews characterized by their affiliation with synagogues or temples, the question still remained as to the choice of denomination.[6] The memberships of Reform temples were selected for several reasons.

Ellman mentions the Conservative movement as one of the "new ethnic forms"[7] for Jews in America. The same can certainly be said of Reform Judaism and the Reform movement. While usually associated with the origins of Reform Judaism in Germany, recent scholarship has pointed to the evolution of Reform Judaism in America as a pragmatic response to uniquely American conditions, and in fact to its initial development independent of the later German ideological influence.[8] The subsequent influx of east European Jews and their later involvement in the Reform movement also became a factor shaping the particular development of Reform Judaism in America in the twentieth century.

Reform Judaism and Reform Jews have been relatively little studied in depth. While two major studies of aspects of Reform Judaism were published in the early seventies,[9] neither was an in-depth examination of communities of Reform Jews and neither focused on issues of ethnicity.

The issue of Jewish density, a focal point of the present research, is often discussed in relation to Orthodox Jews. It has not, however, been examined as a significant variable in the study of Reform Jews. In suburban settings the interaction of cultural and structural features of the group with those of the general American environment is more fluid than in the more segregated urban "ghetto" situation. It is Reform Jews and Reform Judaism that have typically been most concerned with adaptation to the host society.

II. Social Characteristics of the Sample

This section will present a description of the sample in terms of basic social characteristics[10] and an analysis of the interaction among these social characteristics for the respondents themselves, for all males and for all females.[11] The purpose of this description is threefold: to acquaint the reader with a general profile of the sample; to hightlight some of the ways in which the sample is atypical of Jewish populations; and, from that description and analysis to elaborate on the reasons behind the choice of this special population for research

A. Social Characteristics

Of the 238 respondents, 48% are males and 52% are females. Ninety-nine percent of the sample is currently married, with only one percent currently divorced or separated.[12] Eighty-five percent of the respondents have children below eighteen living at home with them. About half of the families have a child or children aged six to ten and two-fifths have children aged 16 to 18, while about 90% have a child or children between the ages of 11 and 15.

Over 95% of the respondents are between the ages of 30 and 59. The median age of both respondents and spouses is 37, while the mean age of the respondents is 44.6. Table 2.1 shows the age breakdown of those aged 30-59 for respondents by sex, as well as that of all males and all females. The overwhelming majority of respondents (90.5%), as well as of all males (90.4%) and all females (92.1%), are second or third generation (Table 2.2).[13]

Table 2.1: Age Groupings of Respondents 30-59
(by Sex), All Males, All Females

Age	respondents				all males	all females
	males	females	total		males	females
30-39	12.8	34.7	24.3		18.9	34.2
40-49	57.8	52.9	55.2		54.8	52.8
50-59	29.4	12.4	20.4		26.3	13.0
column	109	121	230		228	231
totals	47.4	52.6	100%		100%	100%

We are dealing with a very highly educated population in terms of secular education. While for American Jews the percentage with at least some college is 52%[14] and for the 1975 greater Boston sample 69%,[15] 95% of the respondents are in this category of educational attainment (Table 2.3). Even more strikingly, 43% of the respondents (and 54% of all males, 30% of all females) hold a graduate or professional degree. The

Table 2.2: Generation of Respondents
All Males, All Females

Generation	respondents	all males	all females
lst	5.6	6.1	4.0
2nd	41.4	50.2	39.2
3rd	49.1	40.2	52.9
4th	3.9	3.5	4.0
column	232	229	227
totals	100%	100%	100%

comparable figures for American Jews and for the 1975 Boston sample are 18%[16] and 26%[17] respectively.

Occupations of respondents and spouses were rated according to the scale of occupational prestige presented in Treiman.[18] We are clearly dealing with a population which is skewed towards the upper end of the occupational prestige scale (Table 2.4).

Table 2.3: Secular Education of Respondents
All Males, All Females

	respondents	all males	all females
high school or less	5.1	4.7	6.4
some college	16.6	10.2	25.2
completed college	23.4	23.0	25.6
some graduate school	11.5	8.1	12.4
grad. or prof. degree	43.4	54.0	30.3
column	235	235	234
totals	100%	100%	100%

The income of respondents was ascertained in response to the following questionnaire item: "What is the approximate annual gross income of

Table 2.4: Occupational Prestige Ratings of Those
in the Labor Force* for Respondents
All Males, All Females

Occupational Prestige Rating	respondents	all males	all females
34-44	5.5	1.7	7.1
45-54	24.0	15.7	34.2
55-64	40.0	34.9	43.9
65-74	21.5	28.8	11.0
75+	9.0	18.8	3.9
column	200	229	155
totals	100%	100%	100%

* Housewives were omitted from this table.

your household (you and, if applicable, your spouse)?" The sample is clearly also skewed toward the upper end of the income spectrum. Only 5.7% of the respondents report an annual income below $30,000 (Table 2.5). In the income distribution reported for Jews in the greater Boston area in 1975, 61% report income below $20,000 per year.[19] Even adjusting generously for inflation during the intervening period, the high income profile of our respondents is striking.[20]

Table 2.5: Approximate Gross Annual Income of Household

under $30,000	5.7
$30,000 - $50,000	27.8
$50,000 - $70,000	31.4
$70,000 - $90,000	8.8
over $90,000	26.3
column	194
totals	100%

B. Associations among Social Characteristics

As expected, there is a high correlation between age and generation for respondents, all males, and all females. While only one-quarter of the respondents aged 30-39 are first or second generation, nearly 70% of those 50-59 fall into that generational category. The comparable figures for all males are 30.8% and 77.2%, and for all females 21.3% and 69.0%.

Age was not highly correlated with education or occupation. The percentage holding graduate or professional degrees across all three age categories was almost identical for respondents and for all females. For all males, the percentage holding advanced degrees was somewhat lower for the oldest age cohort than for the middle or youngest age groups. At the opposite end of the educational attainment spectrum, these findings are consistent with widely recognized trends among American Jews: 100% of the youngest age cohort has at least some college education, while it is only among the oldest age group that anything approaching a significant percentage did not attend college.

Generation also did not correlate highly with the level of educational attainment or occupational prestige. The most striking – though not surprising – finding was the significant difference between males and females. For the second and third generations, which together comprise over 90% of all males and all females, almost twenty percent more males than females have at least completed college.

The relationship between education and occupation was very strong, with sexual differences once again pronounced. While only 19% of the males and 6% of the females with a college degree or less were at the upper end of the occupational prestige hierarchy, 63% of the males but only 22% of the females with at least some graduate study were similarly situated in terms of occupational prestige (Table 2.6).

To examine correlations of income with other social characteristics, joint measures of the latter were devised for respondents and spouses. This was necessitated by the form in which information on income was gathered, namely, in response to a question asking for the "approximate gross annual income of your *household (you, and if applicable, your spouse)*." (emphasis added)

Table 2.6: Occupational Prestige of All Males
and All Females BY Education

Occupational Prestige Rating	all males low*	high**		all females low	high	
34–64	80.7	37.1		93.9	78.2	
65–75+	19.3	62.9		6.1	21.8	
column	83	143	226	66	87	153***
totals	36.7	63.3	100%	43.1	56.9	100%

Educational Attainment

* low=completed college or less
** high=some graduate study to graduate or professional degree
*** The low N is the result of the elimination of the "housewife" category.

Two-thirds of those couples in which both spouses had high occupational prestige ratings were in the higher income category, while one-third of the couples with one high and one low occupation and one-quarter of those couples in which both spouses had low occupational prestige ratings were also to be found in this upper end of the income scale (Table 2.7). Differences in income among categories of educational attainment were minimal. Income was inversely related to age.

Table 2.7: Income of Household BY Occupation of
Respondent and Spouse

	Occupation both low*	mixed	both high	
< $70,000	74.1	66.7	33.3	
> $70,000	25.9	33.3	66.7	
column	58	60	12	130**
totals	44.6	46.2	9.2	100%

* low=occ. prestige rating of 34–64; high=occ. prestige rating of 65 or more.
** The low N is the result of two factors: couples in which one spouse listed "housewife" as occupation (65 cases) were not included, and the income question was not answered by 44 respondents.

III. Community Background

Liberty is a primarily residential suburb located within easy commuting distance of downtown Boston and close to the high technology industries which line Boston's circumferential highway. Its suburban character is reflected in the fact that single-family homes comprise 90% of all housing in the town.[21] The population of Liberty is overwhelmingly white. Many of its residents are well-educated, fairly affluent, and relatively young, with 41% under the age of twenty and only 8% over sixty-five.

Newington is located just seven miles from downtown Boston. Its population density is more than two and a half times that of Liberty and just over 60% of its housing consists of single-family units.[22] While some of the neighborhoods or "villages" in Newington are also suburban in nature, the City of Newington as a whole is less clearly suburban. Whereas Liberty made the transition directly from a largely agricultural area to a residential "bedroom" community, the early history of Newington as a locale of light manufacturing is still reflected in a few parts of the city. Nonetheless, Newington is considered "one of the finest residential areas in the Metropolitan Area."[23]

The population of Newington, like that of Liberty, is overwhelmingly white. A lower proportion of its residents are as well-educated and as affluent as those in Liberty. The population of Newington is also on the average somewhat older than that of Liberty, with 34% under twenty and 12% over sixty-five.

The first Jews came to Liberty at the turn of the century, the first Jewish congregation was chartered in Liberty in 1911, and its first synagogue dedicated in 1916. Liberty did not have two congregations, however, until 1959. The Jewish population of Liberty decreased in the years prior to World War II. The increase in its Jewish population in the period immediately following the war was one factor leading to the purchase in 1955 of a building to serve as a synagogue-center for Liberty and two nearby towns. The building which had until then housed Liberty's sole Jewish congregation was sold to aid in the purchase of the new synagogue-center building. Services which had been Orthodox were transferred to the new facility and became Conservative.

The emphasis of Liberty's Jews on fitting into the surrounding community continued together with the establishment of the new synagogue-center with its religious services and Hebrew school. Among the activities described as being held in the new building were interfaith meetings; when the High Holiday attendance outgrew the center's facilities, services were conducted in the meeting hall of a local church. The synagogue-center building was likewise used by a newly founded church for Sunday school and services. Not incidentally, the first rabbi hired for the center was then completing a doctorate at Harvard in English literature.

In 1959, there was a split in the synagogue-center membership precipitated by the designation of a committee to select a new rabbi. While one group stayed at the center, hired a Conservative rabbi, and affiliated with the Conservative movement, another group left to hire a Reform rabbi and form Temple Am Shalom.

In the next decade, both congregations prospered as their memberships increased with the influx of new Jewish families to Liberty. They engaged in fund-raising campaigns and built the new buildings which currently house them. There are, however, many Jewish families in the Liberty area who are not members of either temple; it is estimated that approximately half of Liberty's Jews are not affiliated with any synagogue or temple.

Ground-breaking ceremonies for the Temple Am Shalom building took place in 1962. In anticipation of that event, the then president of the congregation wrote: "While we recognize the need for the building, we do not intend to build elaborately or extravagantly. Good taste, rather than extravagance, will guide us..."[24]

Since then, the building has been expanded twice, though its original design and proportions have been faithfully preserved. At the time of the first expansion, insufficient funds were available and a decision was made to increase the number of classrooms in the Temple Am Shalom religious school while delaying the proposed additions to the sanctuary and other facilities. While the latter additions have also been completed within the past few years, the initial choice reflects in very concrete terms the priority placed by the congregation on the Jewish education of its children. In addition to Jewish education, the Am Shalom Arts Institute is a major focus of annual activity, bringing "several times each year Jewish artists and performers of stature who could enrich our Shabbat and in turn relate how their Jewishness affected their art forms."[25]

The rabbi of Temple Am Shalom describes his congregants as having a very high level of secular education. He also feels that they are positively identified as Jews:

> It used to be that the Jews who were moving out to Liberty were thought to be somehow escaping their Jewish identity. I never had that sense at all. I think that it was part of the 1950's move to suburbia and that once the Jews moved here...they wanted to establish their identity as Jews.[26]

He describes Temple Am Shalom as "a synagogue in the best sense of the word - we really are a *beit knesset.*"[27] There are, as noted, many Jews in Liberty who are not affiliated with any Jewish congregation and many who are not as strongly identified as Rabbi Ellis perceives the members of his own congregation to be. In Rabbi Ellis' words:

> That's not to say that there aren't a good many people in the community who are universalists and see affiliation with any Jewish organization as somehow detracting from that universalism. They choose not to be affiliated with a synagogue, to rear their children without any particular Jewish identity. My guess is that for every Jew that's affiliated in Liberty, there's probably another who is not.[28]

Rabbi Ellis feels that while there are two neighborhoods in Liberty that are "fairly heavily" populated with Jews, "by and large the Jewish community is very intermixed neighborhood-wise. When someone comes to me and asks 'Where do the Jews live?,' I have to say everywhere."[29]

Nonetheless, the Jewish presence in Liberty is much less strongly felt than in Newington. Jews do not fundamentally alter Liberty as they do Newington. Further, they do not want to; doing so would decrease one source of its very attractiveness to them, namely, its reputation as an "American" and not a Jewish or ethnic suburb.

The earliest records of Jews living in Newington date from the last third of the nineteenth century. The number of Jewish residents there increased slowly through the early 1900's. As the country emerged from the Depression in the 1930's, Newington's Jewish community began to grow noticeably. The period of greatest growth began around 1950. By the late 1950's, it was estimated that approximately six thousand Jewish families were living in Newington, comprising over twenty percent of its total population. Certain sections of Newington were already then noted for their especially high concentration of Jews.

The accelerating growth of Newington's Jewish community is reflected in the history of its synagogues and temples. The first synagogue building was completed in 1912 and housed an Orthodox congregation. Through the 1920's, many of Newington's Jewish residents maintained their affiliation with synagogues and temples in Boston itself. A second congregation – this one Conservative – was not established until 1935, when the Jewish population of Newington consisted of about five hundred families. The building which presently houses this congregation was built in 1952.

Newington's first Reform congregation was established in 1950 and moved into its present building in 1956. A second Conservative congregation was established in 1952, and a third, much older Conservative congregation moved to Newington later in the same decade. In 1957, an Orthodox synagogue was added to the roll of Newington's synagogues and temples. Newington's second Reform temple, Temple Tikvah, was established in 1963.

In addition to its many synagogues and temples, the Newington Jewish community is served by a veteran community center, built to accommodate the Jewish residents of Newington and two adjacent communities. More recently, Newington was chosen as the site for a major new Jewish community center facility.

In the late 1950's, a prominent local rabbi claimed that "Newington stands for prosperity and success," despite its having a not insignificant proportion of lower-middle class families. He described Newington's Jewish community as follows:

> The Jewish community is generally regarded as well-off, even though there are signs that many Jewish families can be classified no higher economically than lower-middle class. In Newington, as in numerous other old suburbs, there reside *two* classes of Jewish families – those who moved into the suburb in the late 1930's, and the newer suburbanites who appeared beginning in 1946. The former group is generally well-established financially, whereas the second group includes many families who look forward to a better financial status for themselves in the years ahead.[30]

It was primarily this second type of family that in the years following World War II moved into the section of Newington where Temple Tikvah is now located. Single-family homes were made available there for returning veterans at very moderate prices. Since then, other houses, including some of Newington's most expensive homes, have been built in the area.

According to Rabbi Morse of Temple Tikvah, the area "feels like eighty percent Jewish, though it is mixed according to streets."[31] He describes the temple as a "neighborhood temple" with over three-fourths of its members living in the immediate vicinity. The membership of Temple Tikvah, he claims, includes a wide spectrum of economic and social groupings.

Temple Tikvah was founded by a core of people from "traditional backgrounds...ethnically inclined...some very comfortable with Yiddish."[32] While subsequently joined by "people from totally assimilated and classical Reform backgrounds," nonetheless those from more traditional backgrounds "still feel comfortable here because we're not ultra Reform."[33] Rabbi Morse explains:

> We're in the Reform camp ideologically, liturgically, educationally. But we do have certain *minhagim* (customs) that are a reflection of a more traditional background. We wear

kippot (skullcaps); we make use of *talesim* (traditional prayer shawls). My own characteristics are traditional. They know not to ask me to perform an intermarriage.[34]

As in the case of Temple Am Shalom, Jewish education and children generally are a major focus of concern and activity at Temple Tikvah. Its membership takes great pride in their large school and various youth programs, in addition to an adult education program highlighted by a Sunday morning Torah class.

The Jewish population of Newington in 1975 was approximately 22,500.[35] Jews thus comprise approximately 25% of Newington's total population. We must remember, however, that the Jewish population of Newington is far from evenly distributed throughout the city. While there are large sections of Newington with very few Jews, other sections have very high Jewish concentrations.

Estimates of the proportion of Jews in Liberty range from 15–20%; the difference between the estimated proportion of Jews in Newington and Liberty is thus between five and ten percent. The Jews of Liberty are, however, less concentrated within Liberty's population. There are also other factors which serve to make Newington as a whole and especially certain sections a much more Jewish community than Liberty. The first is of course that Newington's total Jewish population is several times larger than that of Liberty. The section of Newington from which Temple Tikvah draws most of its membership is one of the areas more heavily populated by Jews.

In addition, as noted, Jews do not change Liberty in any basic sense as they do Newington. They establish two congregations there, but no other visible Jewish institutions which would create a Jewish milieu or accent the presence of a Jewish community. Rather, they value and respect the character of Liberty as an elite and archetypically "Yankee" community. The character of Liberty is perceived as continuing basically unchanged since its colonial and Revolutionary War heritage.

Though established at the end of the seventeenth century, Newington's colonial past figures much less prominently in its contemporary image.

Newington thus does not evoke associations with a past that is "sacred" in American mythology, and changes in the character of the community have therefore encountered much less opposition. Though also a self-proclaimed elite community, Newington has long been home to a composite of ethnic "newcomers" as well as to old Yankee families. For Jews to also imprint their ethnic stamp on Newington does not violate the very character of the community as it would in Liberty.

Newington's Jewish community stands in a symbiotic relationship with that of a neighboring town which is perhaps the most widely-recognized locale of contemporary Jewish residence in the Boston area. No such relationship ties Liberty with other Jewish communities; Liberty is associated rather with other suburbs that are considered the embodiment of white Protestant communities. Finally, in addition to Newington's numerous synagogues and temples and its association with two Jewish community centers, there are in Newington Jewish butcher shops, bakeries, delicatessens, and other Jewish specialty stores. Such visible signs of Jewish presence are not to be found in Liberty.

Thus, the different perceptions of Jewish residential concentration in Newington and in Liberty presented in this study are grounded in real demographic differences and also reflect the respective historical and institutional development of the two communities.

IV. Differences by Temple

The membership of Temple Am Shalom is slightly older and of lower generational status than that of Temple Tikvah. The differences between the two temple memberships in terms of education are more pronounced (Table 2.8). The relatively high 28% of respondents from Temple Tikvah who hold graduate or professional degrees is actually doubled among respondents from Temple Am Shalom. This ratio holds true for all males (where the percentage holding an advanced degree among members of Temple Am Shalom reaches 69.8%) and rises to 1:2.6 for all females.

The occupational prestige picture of the two temple memberships is a bit more complex (Table 2.9). The membership of Temple Tikvah is more heavily represented in the relatively lower occupational prestige categories.[36] For respondents and for all females, representation in the middle occupational status categories is higher for Temple Am Shalom members, while for all males there is virtual parity between the members of both temples. In the highest occupational prestige categories, there is parity for respondents and all females, while Temple Am Shalom males have a decided edge.

Table 2.8: Educational Attainment of Respondents BY Temple

	Am Shalom	Tikvah	
h.s. or less	3.1	7.5	
some college	10.2	24.3	
compl.college	17.2	30.8	
graduate study	13.3	9.3	
grad/prof deg.	56.3	28.0	
column	128	107	235
totals	54.5	45.5	100%

Table 2.9: Occupational Prestige of Respondents
All Males, All Females BY Temple

Occupational	respondents		all males		all females	
	Am.		Am.		Am.	
Prest. Rating	Sh.	Tikv.	Sh.	Tikv.	Sh.	Tikv.
34–54	22.3	38.6	8.2	28.0	33.3	53.2
55–64	46.4	31.8	36.1	33.6	51.6	32.3
65–75+	31.3	29.5	55.7	38.3	15.1	14.5
column	112	88	122	107	93	62
totals	56.0	44.0	53.3	46.7	60.0	40.0

A more detailed examination of the upper end of the occupational prestige spectrum for all males, however, reveals an important distinction. The advantage accruing to Temple Am Shalom males is actually located in the 75+ occupational prestige range, while there is virtual parity in the 65–74 occupational prestige category. To relate these numerical representations to actual occupations listed by respondents: 1) the males of Temple Am Shalom are more heavily engaged in the free professions

– hence their higher percentage in the 75+ category; 2) the males of Temple Am Shalom are also found in large numbers in the salaried professions, while the males of Temple Tikvah are more heavily engaged in business.

Temple Tikvah households are slightly more heavily represented at either end of the income scale – in the under $50,000 and in the over $70,000 categories – while Temple Am Shalom households are more heavily represented in the middle or $50,000–$70,000 category (Table 2.10)[37]

Table 2.10: Income of Household BY Temple

	Am Shalom	Tikvah	
under $30,000	3.7	8.1	
$30–$50,000	25.9	30.2	
$50–$70,000	38.0	23.3	
$70–$90,000	8.3	9.3	
over $90,000	24.1	29.1	
column	108	86	194
totals	55.7	44.3	100%

V. Social Characteristics as Factor in Choice of Research Population

We are dealing primarily with second and third generation parents of intact families with teenage children living at home. While mention was made earlier of recent changes in the family patterns of American Jews, it is critical not to lose sight of the importance of understanding "conventional" American Jewish families in the rush to focus on more recent rends. It is after all these intact nuclear families that still comprise the mainstream of membership in many of the core institutions and organizations of the American Jewish community.

Our sample is concentrated overwhelmingly towards the upper reaches of educational attainment, occupational prestige, and income. In terms of generation, the sample is fairly representative of American Jews in general and of greater Boston Jews in particular.[38] While their generational representativeness is important, it is this representativeness coupled with their specialness in the educational and occupational spheres which is of most interest.

As Kobrin and Goldscheider[39] suggest, ethnicity should not be viewed as a uniform phenomenon affecting or expressing itself in all segments of a given group in similar fashion. Variables of education, occupation, and place of residence come into play. More specifically, they hypothesize that it is the urban (here their scheme must be amended from "urban" to "suburban" for American Jews), highly educated, and occupationally successful segments of the group that best serve as predictors of change in the group. Sklare bases his choice of research site in *Jewish Identity on the Suburban Frontier* on much the same considerations.[40] Thus, coming from the common pool of American and greater Boston Jews by generation, these respondents and their spouses likely represent the educational, occupational, and residential vanguard of their larger group of origin.

The analysis by temple also reveals findings that recommend study of this research population as potentially yielding important insights on the attitudinal correlates of significant trends affecting the Jewish group in America. While American Jews at or near the high end of the occupational ladder were until recently concentrated primarily in the free professions and in business, there is evidence of increasing movement from these realms into the salaried professions.

The effects on attitudes and identification of moving from a largely Jewish environment of colleagues and clients to an environment suffused with pressure to conform to norms and behavior patterns of a non-Jewish corporation or firm have potentially consequential effects on matters of Jewish ethnicity. The Jewish lawyer in private practice whose clientele consists to a significant degree of other Jews is working in a setting different in meaningful ways from that of the Jewish lawyer in a prestigious "Yankee" law firm or international corporation. The latter is likewise in a very different position from that of the Jewish businessman whose customers, employees, and not unlikely whose suppliers as well, may be fellow Jews.[41]

Finally, the population chosen for study is overwhelmingly comprised of families with children still in their formative years, at critical ages in terms of development of identity. Stage in the life cycle is a crucial factor affecting attitudes and behavior related to identity formation and transmission. Significant attitudes are influenced by consideration of their potential to affect children in desired ways.

Notes

1. Yancey, Ericksen, and Juliani, op. cit., p. 392.

2. Herberg, op. cit., *Protestant, Catholic, Jew*; Andrew Greeley, *The Denominational Society* , Glenview, Illinois: Scott, Foresman, 1972.

3. Marshall Sklare, *Conservative Judaism*, Glencoe, Illinois: Free Press, 1955, pp.35–40.

4. Yisrael Ellman, "The Ethnic Awakening in the United States and Its Influence on Jews," *Ethnicity* 4 (1977): 133–155.

5. It must be stressed, however, that this is not an institutional study of the temples. Rather, as mentioned in the text, the temples serve as institutional focal points around which the communities studied are located.

6. While "denomination" is not fully satisfying as a term to characterize Orthodox, Conservative, and Reform Judaism in the United States, neither is there a fully satisfactory alternative. "Movements" or "branches" are the descriptive alternatives most often used.

7. Ellman, op. cit., p. 144.

8. See, for example, Leon Jick, *The Americanization of the Synagogue, 1820–1870*, Hanover, New Hampshire: University Press of New England, 1976.

9. Theodore I. Lenn, *Rabbi and Synagogue in Reform Judaism*, New York: Central Conference of American Rabbis, 1972; Leonard J. Fein et al., *Reform Is a Verb*, New York: Union of American Hebrew Congregations, 1972. For a recent study of a particular Reform congregation, see Frida Kerner Furman, *Beyond Yiddishkeit: The Struggle for Jewish Identity in a Reform Synagogue*, Albany, New York: State University of New York Press, 1987.

10. The function of social characteristics as a factor in the selection of the specific suburban Reform Jewish communities chosen as a research population are dealt with below. While the social characteristics of the sample could be determined only in the course of the research itself, prior familiarity with the communities involved enabled taking estimates of these characteristics into account in deciding which specific communities to study.

11. "All males" is defined as male respondents and spouses of female respondents; "all females" as female respondents and spouses

44

of male respondents.

12. The description is of the social characteristics of the sample, *not* of the total temple memberships. As a case in point, only 1% of the *sample* is currently divorced or separated; an effort was made to screen out single-parent families which constituted 8% of the Temple Am Shalom and 11% of the Temple Tikvah memberships.

13. Second generation is defined as the first native-born generation. Fred Massarik and Alvin Chenkin, "United States National Jewish Population Study: A First Report," *AJYB* 74 (1973): 277.

15. Floyd J. Fowler, Jr., *1975 Community Survey, A Study of the Jewish Population of Greater Boston,* Boston: Combined Jewish Philanthropies of Greater Boston, 1977, p. 18.

16. Massarik and Chenkin, loc. cit. The graduate study figure there includes all those with post B.A. work and is therefore not strictly comparable. It would compare rather with the 55% of respondents in the present sample with some graduate work or more.

17. Fowler, loc. cit.

18. Donald J. Treiman, *Occupational Prestige in Comparative Perspective,* New York: Academic Press, 1977. As the data upon which the current analysis is based include information on education and income, and are for a specific subgroup within the American population, the Treiman scale of occupational prestige (Standard Scale) was chosen for use rather than the more widely known Duncan Socioeconomic Index of Occupations. As Treiman writes: "...where no information but occupation is available regarding the socioeconomic status of individuals, the Duncan index is preferred precisely because – by virtue of the way it is constructed – it will capture more joint variance with education and income than would a prestige scale. However, *this same attribute may be reason enough to eschew the Duncan scale when other information on the socioeconomic status of individuals is available*, simply to avoid artificially inflated correlations. The main reason for utilizing the Standard Scale (Treiman's)...is that...the prestige hierarchy of occupations is essentially invariant in all populations, *including subgroups within each society.*" (Treiman, op.cit., p.212.) (emphasis added.) To give the reader an idea of the range and rating of the Treiman scale, examples of scores on the Standard Scale for occupations actually

listed by respondents are as follows:

occupation	prestige score
Physician	78*
Lawyer, Trial Lawyer	71
Business Executive	67
Electrical Engineer	65
Artist	57
Sales Manager	52
Computer Programmer	51
Traveling Salesman	47
Automobile Dealer	44
Foreman	39
Sales Clerk	34

*Occupational descriptions and scores are taken from Treiman, op.cit., "Appendix A, Standard International Occupational Prestige Score," pp. 235–260.

19. Fowler, op. cit., p. 46.

20. Although the percentage of non-response was rather high on this sensitive question, the income picture which emerges is likely an accurate representation of the income distribution of the sample. This conclusion is supported by more detailed distributions which emerged from crosstabulations of income by education and occupation for the membership of each temple. These crosstabulations accurately corroborated evidence derived from the actual occupational categories listed by respondents and from other sources that the membership of Temple Am Shalom tends to be concentrated in the free and salaried professions while the membership of Temple Tikvah is relatively more concentrated in the world of business.

21. "City and Town Monographs," Massachusetts Department of Commerce and Development.

22. Ibid.

23. Ibid.

24. "A History of Temple Am Shalom," (pseud.) Mimeographed. 1977.

25. Ibid.

26. Interview with Rabbi Ellis, 10.31.80.

27. Literally, "house of assembly," the traditional term for a synagogue. Though Temple Am Shalom is clearly not a traditional

synagogue with adult prayer and study the focal points of activity, Rabbi Ellis' use of the traditional term is an attempt to convey a felt link with the traditional synagogue as a central institution in the community and a sense that a broad range of activities, religious and social, take place there.

28. Interview with Rabbi Ellis, 10.31.80

29. Ibid.

30. The full reference is not cited here as doing so would clearly reveal Newington's true identity.

31. Interview with Rabbi Morse, 10.23.80.

32. Ibid.

33. Ibid.

34. Ibid.

35. Fowler, op. cit., p. 23.

36. In addition, 40 respondents or spouses of Temple Tikvah and 25 of Temple Am Shalom are "housewives" (63 females and 2 males are included among the 65 "housewives").

37. Examination of the relationships between income, occupation, and education by temple corroborated the categorization of the respective occupational concentrations of the two groups, as well as supporting the validity of the information gathered on income. These crosstabulations showed that: 1) more Am Shalom households in the highest income category are in the higher categories of occupational prestige and educational attainment, representing the free professions; 2) more Am Shalom households in the middle income category are in the higher category of educational attainment and in the lower category of occupational prestige, representing the salaried professions; 3) more Tikvah households in the highest income category are in the lower educational and occupational categories, representing business.

38. From the 1975 Boston study (p.16) we note that 34% of greater Boston Jews are second generation (compared with 40.3% of the present respondents) and that 49% are third generation or later (compared with 51.7% of the present sample).

39. Frances E. Kobrin and Calvin Goldscheider, *The Ethnic Factor in Family Structure and Mobility*, Cambridge, Mass.: Ballinger Press, 1978, p. 2.

40. Sklare and Greenblum, op.cit., pp. 7–9.

41. In addition to the above considerations, there is evidence that the move from business to the salaried professions may have considerable impact on Jewish giving and lay leadership, both of which affect a cornerstone of Jewish ethnic activity and expression, the organized communal structure.

CHAPTER THREE

THE MEMBERSHIPS OF TEMPLE AM SHALOM (LIBERTY) AND TEMPLE TIKVAH (NEWINGTON): A COMPARISON

I. Introduction

As all of the respondents from each temple live in the community in which their temple is located, we are in effect dealing with a comparison of the two communities.

Substantial contrasts exist between the residents of Liberty and of Newington precisely on those measures of Jewish density which form the pivotal analytic variables in this study (Table 3.1). Nearly 90% of the Temple Tikvah members perceive of their community as comprised of half or more Jews, while only 10% of Temple Am Shalom members perceive of their community in similar fashion. The difference in friendship patterns, while less extreme, is also striking: more than eight of ten members of Temple Tikvah report that all or most of their friends are Jews, while less than six of ten Am Shalom members report a similar proportion of Jewish friends.

Thus, analysis by residential and friendship variables will reflect differences between the two temples and communities.

II. Jewish Background by Temple

Primary focus here is on the Jewish background of the respondents themselves; where relevant, variables will also be discussed in terms of combined measures for respondent and spouse.

A significantly higher percentage of Tikvah than of Am Shalom respondents report having grown up in communities where Jews made up half or more of the community population (Table 3.2). While the difference between the two groups in terms of Jewish childhood friends is less striking, the advantage once again goes to Tikvah members.

Tikvah members reported that their friends were a more important early influence on their current level of Jewishness. A higher percentage of

Table 3.1: Current Jewish Density BY Temple

Proportion of Jews in the community	Temple Am Shalom	Temple Tikvah	
all or most	0.8	50.9	
about half	9.4	38.9	
some or fewer	89.8	10.2	
column	128	108	236
totals	54.2	45.8	100%

Proportion of Jewish Friends	Temple Am Shalom	Temple Tikvah	
all or most	57.8	83.5	
half or fewer	42.2	16.5	
column	128	109	237
totals	54.0	46.0	100%

Table 3.2: Background Jewish Density BY Temple

Proportion of Jews in Commu. where Grew Up	Temple Am Shalom	Temple Tikvah	
half or more	41.4	73.1	
some or none	58.6	26.9	
column	128	108	236
totals	54.2	45.8	100%

Proportion of Jewish Friends Growing Up	Temple Am Shalom	Temple Tikvah	
all or most	60.5	71.0	
half or less	39.5	29.0	
column	129	107	236
totals	56.7	45.3	100%

Tikvah than of Am Shalom respondents also felt that their current circle of friends was an important influence on their current level of Jewishness.

More of the Am Shalom respondents report that their parents considered themselves Orthodox, while more of the Tikvah respondents report that their parents considered themselves Conservative or Reform, though the differences are relatively small.

While a slightly higher percentage of Am Shalom respondents reported remembering celebration of Jewish holidays on a regular basis in their parental homes, Tikvah respondents rated their parents' general observance of Jewish ritual and customs while they, the respondents, were growing up slightly higher than did Am Shalom respondents. A higher percentage of Tikvah respondents reported the presence of Jewish magazines or newspapers, lighting candles on Friday evening, and Israeli objects in their parental homes. Virtually the same percentage of respondents of both groups reported their parents keeping kosher (approximately one-third) and having Jewish ceremonial or art objects (approximately one-half).

In terms of Jewish topics discussed in their parental homes, more Tikvah members reported discussions on Israel, more Am Shalom members reported discussions on anti-Semitism, and approximately two-thirds of each group reported discussions on synagogue or other local Jewish affairs.

A slightly higher percentage of members of Tikvah considered both their parental home and their own Jewish education a very important influence on their current level of Jewishness. Examination of that Jewish education in terms of kind and number of years, however, reveals almost no difference between that of each group.

In terms of more current factors influencing the respondents' current level of Jewishness, we have information in two additional areas: temple and rabbi, Israel and the Holocaust.[1] While differences on the importance of the temple were not significant, the contrast between the two memberships with regard to the importance of the rabbi is striking. Whereas less than one-quarter of the Am Shalom respondents felt that the rabbi was among the very important influences on their current level of Jewishness, nearly one-half of the Tikvah respondents expressed similar feelings.[2]

There was little difference between the two temple subsamples on their respective estimation of the importance of Israel as a factor influencing their current level of Jewishness, and virtually no difference in regard to the Holocaust. It is striking that for both temples nearly twice as many respondents considered the Holocaust a very important factor.[3]

III. Attitudes, Perceptions, Identification by Temple

Not only do members of Temple Tikvah have a higher percentage of Jews in their community; they want it that way. On virtually all of a series of measures, the respondents from Temple Tikvah evince a preference for more Jews and express the importance of the Jewish factor more than do the members of Temple Am Shalom.

Over three-fourths of the Tikvah members, nearly 90% of whom perceive their community as at least half Jewish, stated that the proportion of Jews was a positive factor in their choice of their present community, and only 21.7% said that it played no role at all. Less than two-thirds of the Am Shalom members, nearly 90% of whom perceive their community as having only some Jews, claimed that the proportion of Jews played a positive role while 34.9% stated that it played no role at all. Further, while only 7.8% of Am Shalom respondents mentioned the proportion of Jews and non-Jews as one of the two most important factors influencing their choice of community, 18.3% of the Tikvah respondents made similar mention. On the other hand, 35.7% of the members of Temple Am Shalom cited the general attractiveness of the area as one of the two most important bases of their choice of community, while only 19.3% of the members of Temple Tikvah cited this factor.[4]

While more than three-quarters of Am Shalom respondents would react negatively to the prospect of their community becoming an all or almost all Jewish suburb, less than 40% of Tikvah respondents say they would react in similar negative fashion.[5] On a measure combining both the proportion of Jews in the respondents' present community and their reaction to that situation, the difference between Am Shalom and Tikvah members is indeed striking. While 44.9% of the Tikvah respondents said they would like an all or mostly Jewish community, less than 1% of the Am Shalom members expressed the same preference (Table 3.3).

Table 3.3: Proportion Jewish Want Community BY Temple

	Temple Am Shalom	Temple Tikvah	
all or most	0.8	44.9	
around half	36.2	46.7	
some or few	63.0	8.4	
column totals	127	107	234
	54.3	45.7	100%

Faced with the hypothetical prospect of moving, the proportion of Jewish families would be a factor in choosing a new community for 74.4% of Am Shalom respondents and for 86.9% of Tikvah respondents. In the new community, 77.4% of the latter would regard half or more Jews as ideal while 32.1% of the Am Shalom members would feel likewise.

As already noted, the members of Tikvah report having a higher percentage of friends who are Jewish than do the members of Am Shalom. What are the *attitudes* of each group towards the proportion of Jews in one's friendship network? Three measures address this question. The first is from a series of items in which the respondent is asked to rate several behaviors in terms of one's being considered a "good Jew."[6] In response to the item "have mostly Jewish friends," 28.0% of Tikvah respondents considered it desirable while 16.4% of Am Shalom respondents felt likewise. On the other hand, while 80.5% of the Am Shalom members felt it "makes no difference," 65.4% of the Tikvah members expressed this feeling.

We are faced here not only with a contrast between the two temples, but also with a rather curious situation. While less than 1% of the Tikvah members feel it is essential to have mostly Jewish friends in order to be considered a "good Jew," only 28.0% consider it desirable, and 65.4% feel it makes no difference, fully 83.5% of these same respondents report having mostly Jewish friends. Even for Am Shalom members, over 80%

of whom feel it makes no difference, well over 50% also report having mostly Jewish friends.

One could attempt to explain this apparent inconsistency between attitude and behavior in terms of more frequent contact with other Jews, habit, and other such factors increasing the likelihood of homogeneous Jewish friendship networks. This, however, would still not fully account for the very high percentage of Tikvah respondents who report having mostly Jewish friends despite their feeling that it is not essential and not even very desirable in terms of their being considered good Jews. Further, such an explanation would mask a rather important dichotomy between attitude and behavior which operates in this and related spheres among these respondents and among American Jews in general.

This apparent paradox can be seen as evidence that while Jews express Jewish preferences through their actions,[7] they nonetheless accept the American creed of the equality of all with its behavioral implications *on an ideological level*. Asked directly, in the second measure of attitudes towards friendship patterns, "what proportion of the friends of an American Jew should be Jewish?," only 13.7% of Am Shalom and 30.8% of Tikvah respondents answered "most" while no one of either group answered "all." While 15.6% of Am Shalom respondents and a mere 3.7% of Tikvah respondents have only "some" Jewish friends, 67.0% of the former and 41.1% of the latter express the opinion that an American Jew should have "some" or "few" or that it "doesn't matter." Given the proportion of Jews in the population, these latter situations would more closely approximate the results were the process of selecting friends truly random from an ethnic standpoint, even taking into account such factors as Jewish geographical concentration.

The third measure of attitudes on friendship patterns has to do with children. We may expect a lessening of the "equality of all" ideology and a concomitant increase in the particularistic Jewish response given the concern with transmission of identity to children and with endogamous marriage. Indeed this is precisely what we find. While only 13.7% of the Am Shalom members feel that most of the friends of an American Jew should be other Jews, 45.7% say that it is important to them that most of their children's friends be Jewish. While there are again significant differences between the two memberships, the pattern of increased importance attached to the Jewish friendship pattern of children holds for Tikvah members as well: 30.8% feel that most of the friends of an American Jew should be Jewish and 70.0% want most of their children's friends to be Jewish.

Despite both the behavioral and attitudinal differences between the two groups in terms of friendship patterns, there is a striking similarity in terms of the content of interaction with Jewish friends. For more than seven of ten members of both temples, "Jewish interests and occasions" figure to only some or little extent in their interactions with their Jewish friends. Thus despite their actually having Jewish friends in proportions far beyond both the representation of Jews in the population and the ideal friendship pattern which they express, it is clearly not the desire for explicitly Jewish content which motivates such associational interaction. Rather, the respondents tend to fill the comfortable framework of Jewish friendship networks with Jewish variations on the cultural and leisure-time contents associated with and seen as appropriate to their general class position.[8]

Members of Temple Tikvah viewed anti-Semitism[9] in the United States as a more serious problem than did members of Temple Am Shalom. While almost none of the respondents from either temple felt it was not a problem at all, 15.7% of Tikvah members and 6.3% of Am Shalom members thought it was an extremely serious problem, 48.1% of Tikvah and 32.3% of Am Shalom members thought it to be a fairly serious problem, and 36.1% of Tikvah members but 60.6% of Am Shalom members felt it to be only a moderate problem.

Differences also appeared in the strongest categories of reaction to a prospective intermarriage of one's child. More of the Tikvah respondents would feel very negatively toward and would strongly oppose a prospective intermarriage (Table 3.4). In the "how would you feel" reaction, the difference fades if one takes into account both of the negative categories and not a single respondent from either temple claimed they would react positively to such a situation. Differences do remain, however, in the "which would you most likely do?" reaction to intermarriage. The total "opposing-discouraging" response is larger for Tikvah than for Am

Shalom members. While a not insignificant proportion of both groups would "accept" such a proposed intermarriage, more of the Am Shalom members would do so.

Table 3.4: Reaction to Intermarriage BY Temple
"If a child of yours were to consider marrying
a non-Jew: a. how would you most likely *feel*
about it?

	Temple Am Shalom	Temple Tikvah	
very negative	34.9	49.5	
somewhat negative	58.9	42.2	
no difference	6.2	8.3	
positive	0.0	0.0	
column	129	109	238
totals	54.2	45.8	100%

"If a child of yours were to consider marrying
a non-Jew: b. which would you most likely *do*?

	Temple Am Shalom	Temple Tikvah	
strongly oppose	6.3	17.6	
discourage	46.9	50.9	
be neutral	16.4	12.0	
wouldn't mind	2.3	0.9	
accept	28.1	18.5	
column	128	108	236
totals	54.2	45.8	100%

If we examine the reasons expressed by respondents for feeling negatively towards a prospective intermarriage, we note the following: while a similar proportion of the respondents from each temple mention "difficulties in marriage," nearly twice as many Am Shalom members mention the threat to Judaism. Apparently, Tikvah members feel more confident that Judaism will survive the threat posed by intermarriage and therefore choose to express their opposition in other terms.[10] This difference is perhaps also related to the perception of living as a majority or at least equal component part of the population of one's community rather than as a distinct minority as in the case of Am Shalom members.

The responses to a series of questions on the importance of various factors in a "good Jewish education" (Table 3.5) reveal one key to the Tikvah - Am Shalom differences. The higher percentage of response of the Tikvah members regarding traditional observances, commitment to the Jewish people, defense against anti-Semitism, and feeling for Israel may be understood as evidence of their greater acceptance of Jewish particularism.

Table 3.5: Good Jewish Education BY Temple

"In your opinion, how important is each of the following in a good Jewish education?":

	"very important"	
	Temple Am Shalom	Temple Tikvah
teaching children traditional observances	51.2	67.9
strengthening commitment to the Jewish people	44.4	49.5
developing a strong defense against anti-Semitism	40.5	54.2
developing a strong feeling for Israel	26.0	38.5

Hanukkah and Passover were almost universally observed in some form by members of both groups. In terms of the reasons behind observance of the latter holiday, Tikvah members tended to stress the religious and national aspects more than Am Shalom members, while providing an occasion for a family gathering was the most important factor for both groups. In terms of Sabbath observance, about one-half of each group lights candles, but more Am Shalom members than Tikvah members say the *kiddush*, the traditional blessing over the Sabbath wine.[11] Almost half of the members of Temple Tikvah and a bit over one-third of the Am Shalom members say that their observance of Jewish ritual and customs has increased over the past five years.

Respondents were asked to rate the importance of a series of items in terms of why they celebrate Jewish holidays or observe Jewish customs. "Jewish tradition/culture" figures much more prominently than "Jewish law/ commandments" as a motivating force for all respondents: 98.3% cited the former and only 46.3% the latter as important. However, more Tikvah than Am Shalom respondents consider the law/commandment dimension important. The only item with equal or greater appeal than Jewish tradition/culture was "to transmit Jewishness to my children": 98.7% of all respondents cited this factor as important.[12]

Respondents were asked to rate how Jewish they consider themselves, their spouses and their parents, as well as how Jewish they would like their children to be ("hopes") and how Jewish they think their children will actually be ("expectations"). Uniformly across these five items, more Tikvah members chose 4 (on a scale of 0 to 5, with 0 the least and 5 the most) and more Am Shalom members chose 5. Based on evidence of more Jewish behavior and attitudes among Tikvah members, higher standards or criteria of the latter likely account for this pattern of response. Examination of the means for each of these variables (Table 3.6) shows clearly that although the means for Temple Am Shalom respondents are consistently slightly higher,[13] differences are in all cases extremely small.

What is striking, of course, is that expectations for children are lower than hopes and lower than the ratings of self, spouse, and parents, which exhibit only the slightest decrease from the preceding to the present generation.

Finally, on a series of questions designed to test identification with the Jewish group, a slightly higher percentage of Tikvah members generally showed such identification (Table 3.7). On the first two items, "I feel closer to other Jews than to other Americans" and "I feel a greater sense of responsibility to other Jews than to other Americans," more Temple Tikvah members agree.

Table 3.6: Respondent's Rating of the
Jewishness of Self, Spouse,
Parents, Hopes and Expectations for
Children BY Temple

	mean scores	
	Temple Am Shalom	Temple Tikvah
self	3.39	3.36
spouse	3.31	3.23
parents	3.43	3.37
hopes	3.57	3.51
expectations	2.98	2.94

Table 3.7: Identification BY Temple

	feel closer to Jews than Americans		greater responsi- bility to Jews		negative comment not personal offense	
	Am Sh.	Tikv.	Am Sh.	Tikv.	Am Sh.	Tikv.
strongly agree	25.0	35.2	13.5	24.3	0.0	3.7
agree	53.9	49.1	56.3	50.5	3.9	7.4
disagree	19.5	15.7	27.8	24.3	51.6	40.7
disagree strongly	1.6	0.0	2.4	0.9	44.5	48.1
column totals	128 54.2	108 45.8	126 54.1	107 45.9	128 54.2	108 45.8

The difference shifts in favor of the members of Temple Am Shalom in the "disagree" category of the item "When I hear a negative comment about Jews, I usually *do not* take personal offense." Though they do not necessarily perceive of Jews in general or of themselves in particular primarily as a minority group, Am Shalom respondents are clearly aware of their actual minority status in their community. This may account for their greater sensitivity expressed on the negative measure of identification. It should be noted that, while identifying somewhat less strongly than Tikvah members, Am Shalom members do identify with the Jewish group, their relative aversion to particularism notwithstanding.

IV. Summary

What, then, have we discovered about the members of Temple Tikvah, who perceive living in a more Jewish community and having more Jewish friends, in contrast to the members of Temple Am Shalom?

The members of Temple Tikvah have a slightly more Jewish background than do the members of Temple Am Shalom. The preference of Tikvah members for a more Jewish community seems to reflect their having grown up more so than Am Shalom members in such communities.

Both memberships identify strongly with the Jewish group. The difference between them is one of degree within that identification. Tikvah members are more, and Am Shalom members less, accepting of particularism. This was demonstrated in a series of attitudes and is reflected in their choice of community.

The qualification which must be added to the Am Shalom members' relative aversion to particularism is in relation to the transmission of Jewishness to children and the Jewish composition of children's friendship networks. This may be seen as an extension of the great concern noted on the part of both groups with the issue of intermarriage. The importance of transmission of Jewishness to children is also very much in evidence in the reasons given for Jewish observance and celebration.

While evidence regarding the central research questions posed earlier will come in the course of the direct analysis of background, density, and attitudinal measures, some preliminary indications do emerge from this comparison of the two temple memberships.

The members of Temple Tikvah perceive living in situations of higher Jewish residential concentration and having a higher percentage of Jews among their friends. They also report having more Jewish background than the members of Temple Am Shalom. Jewish factors were reported as having played a larger role in the Tikvah members' choice of their current community. Most strikingly, Tikvah members expressed stronger Jewish attitudes in a series of measures relating to residential and associational concentration, identification with the Jewish group, anti-Semitism, and intermarriage.

Thus the preliminary indication is that Jewishness is still a factor in residential and associational choices especially among the more highly identified, that differences in some important attitudinal dimensions are associated with differences in current Jewish density, and that differences in both attitudes and current Jewish density are associated with differences in Jewish background.

While differences between the two memberships along the critical dimension of current Jewish density prompted the preceding analysis by community, there is sufficient overall similarity between the two groups to allow their treatment in the aggregate for the analysis of associations among background, density, and attitudes. It is important to keep in mind, however, that analysis by categories of current Jewish density reflects differences between the two communities.

Notes

1. Temple and rabbi, Israel and Holocaust, were grouped together for two reasons: 1) the association of the components within each pair in terms of their place and role in American Jewish life and 2) their high loadings in respective factors in a factor analysis executed on a series of Jewish background variables (temple and rabbi, .87 and .85 respectively on one factor; Israel and Holocaust, .66 and .68 respectively on a second factor).

2. Rather than speculate on the meaning of this finding and whether it relates to idiosyncratic differences between the two rabbis and the interaction of what they bring to their role with the particular needs of their respective congregants, it is mentioned here as a suggestive path for further investigation.

3. Once again, a provocative line of inquiry is suggested as to whether this substantial contrast stems from specific programmatic emphases within the two temples or can be related to more general trends for similar populations.

4. Neither of these two considerations, however, approached the importance of the quality of public schools as an influence in choice of community: 80.6% of Am Shalom members and 81.7% of Tikvah members listed this criterion as one of the two most important factors. The convenience of commute to work also figured significantly in the choice of community, listed by 33.3% of Am Shalom members and by 33.0% of Tikvah members as one of the two most important factors. Thus, while not explicitly Jewish themes played a major role for both groups in their respective choice of community, the Jewish aspect of community composition loomed as a larger consideration for members of Tikvah than for members of Am Shalom.

5. We should of course note that Tikvah members live in a community which 50.9% of them consider already mostly Jewish, while less than 1% of Am Shalom members live in such a community. The different percentages of negative reaction, however, do reinforce the respective preferences expressed by residents of the two communities.

6. The "good Jew" questions were devised by Marshall Sklare for his study of Lakeville. See "The Image of the Good Jew in Lakeville" in Sklare and Greenblum, op.cit., pp. 321-332.

7. The Jewish preference in this instance is based primarily on feelings of comfort and compatibility. See "The Friendship Ties of Lakeville Jews" in Sklare and Greenblum, op.cit., pp. 269-290.

8. For a discussion of the intersection of class and ethnicity in regard to social participation and cultural behavior, see Gordon, op.cit, pp. 51-54.

9. Perceptions as to the seriousness of anti-Semitism are included among the attitudinal variables examined in part due to the critical role which such perceptions have played in the Jewish psyche and in the nature of Jewish interaction with the larger societies in which Jews have lived. (This is of course in addition to the role actually played by the phenomenon of anti-Semitism itself.) Whatever its outward manifestation in the American setting, anti-Semitism continues to play a role in the inner life of the American Jew. Slightly over half of the total sample considers anti-Semitism at least a fairly serious problem in the United States.

10. If this supposition about the differential estimation of the ability of Judaism to survive intermarriage is true, the difference may be based on the respective experience of the two groups. It is likely that Am Shalom members are somewhat more exposed to intermarriage and, although there are several cases of intermarried couples in Temple Am Shalom where the non-Jewish spouse (whether converted or not) is an active member of the temple, through a process of residential self-selection on the part of the intermarried couples, one is less likely to see the effects of intermarriage leading to an estrangement from Judaism in a heavily Jewish community such as Newington than in a less heavily Jewish community such as Liberty.

11. The higher percentage of Am Shalom members who say *kiddush* may be the result of particular emphases in the respective temples. However, in the chapters which follow, a higher level of observance is generally associated with *lower* current and background Jewish residential concentration and *less* Jewish attitudes. This may in turn be a function of the particular population studied or the limited and widely observed nature of the specific observances measured. The finding is nonetheless suggestive, and implies that the normal assumption that higher observance is associated with more Jewish background and is an indication of higher identifica-

tion bears careful scrutiny.

12. Further, it is important to 81.1% of Am Shalom respondents and 92.3% of Tikvah respondents to celebrate Jewish holidays or observe Jewish customs in terms of "the general values they represent." The universalistic elements of Jewish observances and celebrations are important to Tikvah members, despite intimations of greater particularism on their part. This supports Sklare's claim that one of the criteria of retention of ritual is that it be "capable of effective redefinition in modern terms" (Sklare, *America's Jews*, op. cit., p.114).

13. A higher score indicates a higher position on the scale.

CHAPTER FOUR

THE RELATION BETWEEN CURRENT JEWISH DENSITY AND BACKGROUND

I. Social Characteristics

Is there a significant relationship between current Jewish density and social characteristics? As both spouses can potentially influence choice of community and friends, the social characteristics presented here are combined measures for both respondent and spouse.[1]

A. Proportion of Jews in the Community

The younger the respondent and spouse, the more Jewish their community. While 51.9% of the younger group live in a setting in which Jews comprise half or more of the population, 45.3% of the middle group and 41.4% of the older group are similarly situated residentially.[2]

Possible explanations for this association must be sought beyond consideration of the two communities in isolation. One interpretation would take into account the distribution of Jews in the greater Boston metropolitan area. Young families desiring a high concentration of Jews have rather few communities from which to choose. They have been able to find accommodation for their residential preferences in the section of Newington from which Temple Tikvah draws a substantial proportion of its membership, an area with a core of small single-family homes. By contrast, young families in search of a community in which Jews comprise only "some or few" of the population have a much broader range of choice in the suburban environs of Boston, including several communities in the western suburban-exurban area. The latter are therefore less likely to be concentrated specifically in Liberty.

Similarly, the higher the generation of the couple, the higher the proportion of Jews in the community. Whereas 58.9% of the couples in which both spouses are third generation live in the more Jewish communities, the same is true of only 43.7% of those in which at least one spouse is second generation. The association between generation and residential concentration is apparently a function of the high correlation between

65

age and generation.

The higher the educational attainment level of the couple, the lower the proportion of Jews in their community (Table 4.1). Only about one-quarter of those households in which both spouses have at least some graduate education live in a situation of high Jewish residential concentration, whereas over 70% of those in which neither spouse has attended graduate or professional school do so.

Table 4.1: Proportion of Jews in the Community
BY Education of Respondent and Spouse

	low*	mixed hi/lo	high**	
half or more	72.9	46.2	24.4	
some or few	27.1	53.8	75.6	
column	70	78	82	230
totals	30.4	33.9	35.7	100%
gamma 0.60				

* low=both spouses high school or less to
completed college
** high=both spouses some graduate school or
graduate/professional degree

Liberty – described by its residents as having only some or few Jews – is well known for its disproportionate attraction of the very highly educated. It is said that the Reform temple there has more doctors – both medical and Ph.D.'s – per capita than any other Reform temple in the United States. Beyond the particular idiosyncrasies of the specific community involved, we are apparently witness to one manifestation of the effect of higher education in promoting a more "cosmopolitan" set of preferences.

In terms of occupational prestige, the group with the highest representation in the more Jewish community category was that in which one spouse worked outside the home while the other's occupation was listed as "housewife." As the same relationship was found in regard to the proportion of friends Jewish (see below), one is led to speculate about the importance of Jewish density when one spouse is not engaged in the labor force but rather has more time to spend at home, in the community and perhaps with friends.

Fewer than four in ten couples in which at least one spouse is in the high occupational prestige category and the other is also in the labor force are in the high Jewish residential concentration category (Table 4.2). The same is true for more than six in ten of those couples in which one spouse is a housewife.

Table 4.2: Proportion of Jews in the Community
BY Occupational Prestige of
Respondent and Spouse

	housewife and...	both low*	both high or mixed hi/lo**	
half or more	63.9	45.6	38.1	
some or few	36.1	54.4	61.9	
column	61	68	84	213
totals	28.6	31.9	39.4	100%
gamma 0.33				

* low=34–64
** high=65 or more

The middle income group was least represented in the more Jewish community category. We noted previously that 38% of the Am Shalom members, but only 23.3% of the Tikvah members are in this middle income category.

B. Proportion of Jews among Friends

Whereas younger couples live in the more Jewish community, older couples reported having slightly higher proportions of Jewish friends. There was no difference in terms of the proportion of friends Jewish by generation.

Education was found once again to be inversely related to the Jewish density variable. Over three-fourths of those couples in which both spouses hold a college degree or less have all or mostly Jewish friends, while approximately 65% of those couples in which at least one spouse has at least some graduate education have all or mostly Jewish friends (Table 4.3). The apparent universalistic-cosmopolitan effect of high secular education is once again in evidence.

Table 4.3: Proportion of Jews among Friends
BY Education of Respondent and Spouse

	low	mixed hi/lo	high	
all or most	78.6	65.4	64.6	
half or fewer	21.4	34.6	35.4	
column	70	78	82	230
totals	30.4	33.9	35.7	100%
gamma 0.21				

Findings on occupation and friends (Table 4.4) parallel those on occupation and community. It is the couples in which one spouse is a housewife that are most heavily represented in the higher Jewish friends category.

There is virtually no difference among income categories in regard to proportion of Jews among friends.

Table 4.4: Proportion of Jews among Friends BY
Occupational Prestige of Respondent
and Spouse

	housewife and...	both low	both high or mixed hi/lo	
all or most	78.7	63.2	67.1	
half or fewer	21.3	36.8	32.9	
column	61	68	85	214
totals	28.5	31.8	39.7	100%
gamma 0.16				

C. Summary

Those living in communities perceived as half or more Jewish tend to be younger and of higher generational status. They have lower levels of educational attainment and occupational prestige, and are located at either end of the income spectrum. Among these social characteristic background factors, the education dimension was found to correlate most highly with the proportion of Jews in the community, as is seen in the summary statistical table (Table 4.5).

Those who have a higher proportion of Jewish friends tend to be somewhat older and in the lower category of educational attainment, and to consist of couples in which one spouse is a housewife. Differences in generation and income were not associated with differences in the proportion of Jews among friends.

Two points should be stressed. Overall, secular education appears to be the social characteristic most highly related to the Jewish density variables. We should therefore be aware of education as an intervening variable and as a potential confounding factor in the relationship between Jewish background, current Jewish density, and attitudes. Second, in comparing the two Jewish density measures – with each social characteristic held constant – more respondents and spouses report having a high proportion of Jewish friends than a high proportion of Jews in their community.

Table 4.5: Summary Statistical Table
Jewish Density and Social
Characteristics*

A. Proportion of Jews in the Community BY:

respondent and spouse:	gamma
AGE	-0.14
EDUCATION	0.60
OCCUPATIONAL PRESTIGE	0.33
INCOME (of household)	0.11

B. Proportion of Jews among Friends BY:

respondent and spouse:	
AGE	0.09
EDUCATION	0.21
OCCUPATIONAL PRESTIGE	0.16
INCOME (of household)	0.02

*selected crosstabulations

II. Jewish Background

Here we will focus mainly on the Jewish background of the respondent only, as information on that of the spouse was collected on only two variables. However, while in the previous section we were limited to speaking of correlations rather than causal relationships, here we are in the fortunate position of being able to consider at least the possibility of causality as the time sequence involved is clear.

The respondent's reported Jewish background was operationally defined as comprised of three components:
1) The early environment outside the parental home, i.e., proportion of Jews in the community in which the respondent grew up and proportion of Jews among the respondent's childhood friends;
2) Aspects of the Jewishness of the parental home including: parents' self-definition as Orthodox, Conservative, or Reform; parents' general level of observance; items present or discussed in the parents' home; and the importance of the parental home as an early influence on the respondent's current level of Jewishness;
3) The respondent's Jewish education and its importance as an early influence on current level of Jewishness.

Is current Jewish density related in a significant way to factors in the Jewish background of the respondent?

A. Proportion of Jews in the Community

While 65.9% of those who reported growing up in a community with "half or more" Jews currently live in a similar community, only 22.3% of those who reported growing up in a community which was less than half Jewish currently live in a community where Jews are half or more of the population (Table 4.6).

A less striking but nonetheless strong association was found between the Jewish composition of the respondent's current community and the proportion of Jews among the respondent's childhood friends. (As will be seen below, the strongest relationship in terms of friends was between current friends and friends growing up, as it is above between current community and the community in which the respondent grew up.) While just over half of those respondents who report growing up with all or mostly Jewish friends currently live in the more Jewish type of community, the same is true of only thirty-seven percent of those who report growing up with "half or fewer Jewish friends" (Table 4.6).

Table 4.6: Proportion of Jews in the
Community BY Background Jewish
Density

	Proportion Jews where Respondent Grew Up			Proportion Jews among Respondent's Childhood Friends		
	half or more	some or none		all or most	half or fewer	
half or more	65.9	22.3		51.0	37.0	
some or few	34.1	77.7		49.0	63.0	
column	132	103	235	153	81	234
totals	56.2	43.8	100%	65.4	34.6	100%
	gamma 0.74			gamma 0.28		

A somewhat higher proportion of respondents whose parents identified as Orthodox or Conservative than of respondents whose parents identified as Reform currently live in communities that are half or more Jewish. There was, however, no difference between those whose parents identified as Orthodox and those whose parents identified as Conservative.

The level of observance of the respondent's parents while the respondent was growing up was also found to be positively related to the proportion of Jews in the respondent's current community (Table 4.7). In this instance, we do have information for both respondent and spouse: the association is indeed strengthened when a combined measure for the observance of parents of respondent and spouse is used.

Respondents were asked which among a series of items they remembered

Table 4.7: Proportion of Jews in the
Community BY Observance of
Respondent's Parents, Observance of
Parents of Respondent and Spouse

	Parents of Respondent			Parents of Respondent and Spouse			
	high*	low**		high	mixed	low	
half or more	52.3	39.4		61.2	44.2	28.6	
some or few	47.7	60.6		38.8	55.8	71.4	
column	132	104	236	85	95	56	236
totals	55.9	44.1	100%	36.0	40.3	23.7	100%
	gamma 0.25			gamma 0.40			

*high=1-3 on a scale of 1-6, with 1 highest
**low=4-6 on a scale of 1-6, with 6 lowest

from their parents' home. The list of items consisted of "celebration of Jewish holidays on a regular basis, presence of Jewish magazines or newspapers, keeping kosher, lighting candles on Friday evening, Jewish ceremonial or art objects, and Israeli objects."[3] Slightly more of those who reported growing up in homes with such Jewish content currently live in more Jewish communities.

Respondents were further asked which of a series of topics they remember being discussed in their parents' home. The list of topics included "Israel, anti-Semitism, and synagogue or other local Jewish affairs."[4] Once again, the Jewish content of the parental home is positively associated to a slight degree with current Jewish residential concentration.

Respondents rated the importance of their parental home as an early influence affecting their current level of Jewishness. A higher proportion of those who considered their parental home an important influence currently live in communities perceived as half or more Jewish (Table 4.8).

Table 4.8: Proportion of Jews in the Community BY
Importance of Parental Home as Influence on
Respondent's Current Level of Jewishness

	important	unimportant	
half or more	48.2	33.3	
some or few	51.8	66.7	
column	195	33	228
totals	85.5	14.5	100%
gamma 0.30			

A positive relationship was found between the proportion of Jews in the
current community and the respondent's evaluation of the importance
of Jewish education as an influence on his/her current level of Jewishness. The relationship between the level of Jewish education (measured
by kind of education and number of years) and the proportion of Jews
in the respondent's community was more complex. For the respondents
themselves, there was very little difference between the high and low
Jewish educational groups. (The minor difference that exists shows an
inverse relationship.) This contrast between *level* of Jewish education
and the *importance attributed* to Jewish education as a lasting influence highlights the fact that the two – one a quantitative measure and
the other more a qualitative evaluation – are not necessarily strongly
related.[5]

When a combined measure of Jewish education for respondent and spouse
is taken into account, it is the couples in which one spouse has a high
Jewish education and one a low Jewish education that are least represented in the more Jewish community category.

B. Proportion of Jews among Friends

The relationship between Jewish background and proportion of Jewish friends is less clear than that between Jewish background and the
proportion of Jews in the community.

The only Jewish background dimension highly associated with the proportion of Jews among respondents' current friends was the respondents' childhood friends. Both the proportion of Jews among childhood friends and the importance of friends as an early factor affecting the respondent's current level of Jewishness had stronger positive relationships to the proportion of current friends Jewish than did any other Jewish background factor.

While 77.8% of those who grew up with all or mostly Jewish friends currently have a similar proportion of Jewish friends, only 56.1% of those who grew up with "half or fewer" Jewish friends currently have a mostly Jewish friendship network (Table 4.9).

Table 4.9: Proportion of Jews among Current
Friends BY Childhood Friends

	Childhood Friends		
Current	all or most	half or fewer	
all or most	77.8	56.1	
half or fewer	22.2	43.9	
column	153	82	235
totals	65.1	34.9	100%
gamma 0.47			

	Importance of Childhood Friends as Influence on Current Level of Jewishness		
Current	important	unimportant	
all or most	74.3	60.7	
half or fewer	25.7	39.3	
column	144	84	228
totals	63.2	36.8	100%
gamma 0.30			

Three-fourths of those who consider their childhood friends an important influence on their current level of Jewishness currently have all or mostly Jewish friends; the same is true of only sixty percent of those who do not consider their childhood friends an important influence on their current level of Jewishness (Table 4.9).

There was almost no difference in the proportion of current friends Jewish according to parent's self-identification or the importance of the parental home as an early influence affecting the respondent's current level of Jewishness, though on these measures the minimal differences were in the expected direction. Small inverse relationships were found between proportion of Jewish friends and the presence of Jewish objects and discussions of Jewish topics in the parental home.

The only Jewish education measure that bore a significant relationship to the proportion of Jews among the respondent's current friends was the combined measure for the Jewish education of the respondent and spouse. As with the proportion of Jews in the community, it was the group in which one spouse has a high Jewish education and one a low Jewish education that was in the least Jewish position (Table 4.10).

Table 4.10: Proportion of Jews among Friends
BY Jewish Education of Respondent
and Spouse

	high	mixed	low	
all or most	85.7	66.7	71.0	
half or fewer	14.3	33.3	29.0	
column	21	42	31	94
totals	22.3	44.7	33.0	100%
gamma 0.19				

C. Summary

The proportion of Jews in the community in which the respondent grew up and among the respondent's friends while growing up, and the Jewishness of the respondent's parental home were positively associated with the proportion of Jews in the community in which the respondent currently lives. The relationship between the Jewish education dimension and current Jewish residential concentration was less clearcut.

While several Jewish background factors are positively associated with the Jewish composition of the respondent's current community, a narrower range of Jewish background factors – particularly Jewish friends while growing up – exhibits the same relationship with the Jewish composition of the respondent's current friendship network.

These findings indicate that selected differences in Jewish background are in fact associated with differences in current residential and friendship patterns. Background Jewish density and the Jewishness of the parental home are positively associated with current Jewish residential concentration; background associational concentration is similarly related to current friendship patterns. Moreover, as is evident in the summary table (Table 4.11), we note in particular the tendency to replicate background residential patterns in current patterns of residential concentration and to a lesser degree to replicate background friendship patterns in current patterns of associational concentration.

Table 4.11: Summary Statistical Table
Jewish Density and Jewish
Background*

A. Proportion of Jews in the Community BY:

respondent:	gamma
PROPORTION JEWS IN COMMUNITY GROWING UP	0.74
PROPORTION JEWS AMONG FRIENDS GROWING UP	0.28
SELF-DEFINITION OF PARENTS	0.09
PARENTS' OBSERVANCE	0.25
PARENTS' OBSERVANCE RESPONDENT AND SPOUSE	0.40
PRESENCE OF JEWISH OBJECTS PARENTAL HOME	0.17
DISCUSSION OF JEWISH TOPICS PARENTAL HOME	0.11
IMPORTANCE PARENTAL HOME EARLY INFLUENCE	0.30
JEWISH EDUCATION:	
Respondent	-0.05
Respondent and Spouse	-0.02
Importance as Early Influence	0.15

B. Proportion of Jews among Friends BY:

respondent:	
PROPORTION JEWS AMONG FRIENDS GROWING UP	0.47
IMPORTANCE FRIENDS AS EARLY INFLUENCE	0.30
JEWISH EDUCATION: Respondent and Spouse	0.19

*selected crosstabulations

Notes

1. The relationship between current Jewish density and the social characteristics of other subgroups in the sample (e.g., respondents only, all males, all females) were also tested. In general, it was found that these relationships were similar in both direction and intensity to those between current Jewish density and the social characteristics of the respondent and spouse. As explained in Appendix A, one spouse in each household was selected as the respondent; information on selected background characteristics of the other spouse was reported by the respondent on the survey instrument.

2. The older group consists of those couples in which both spouses are 50-59, or one is 50-59 and the other 40-49; the middle group, both spouses 40-49; and the younger group, both spouses 30-39, or one 30-39 and one 40-49. Also, we remember that the membership of Temple Tikvah tends to be somewhat younger than that of Temple Am Shalom.

3. A factor analysis showed that the responses on these items were highly related and that the "Israeli objects" item had the highest loading on this factor (.85). The "Israeli objects" item will therefore represent the presence of Jewish items in succeeding analyses.

4. A factor analysis showed that the responses on these items were also highly related and that the responses on the "Israel" item again had the highest loading on this factor (.85). The "Israel" item will therefore represent discussion of Jewish topics in succeeding analyses.

5. For more on this distinction, see the comments in the section of Chapter Nine dealing with the Summary and Interpretation of Profiles.

CHAPTER FIVE

THE RELATION BETWEEN ATTITUDES AND JEWISH DENSITY

I. Introduction

In analyzing the relationship between current Jewish density and attitudes, Jewish density will be treated as an independent variable and the attitudinal measures as dependent variables. We must, however, remember that we are dealing with correlational rather than causal relationships.

The attitudinal measures examined were selected to reflect major component elements of ethnicity:
1) the consciousness of group membership ("group belonging and identification");
2) the distinction between group members and others ("particularism", "anti-Semitism", and "chosenness");
3) aspects of the content held in common by group members ("Israel" and "observance")[1] ;
4) the element of continuity ("hopes and expectations for the Jewishness of one's children" and "the Jewishness of a hypothetical camp setting for one's children"); and
5) the dynamics of group maintenance, through endogamy ("intermarriage") and support of Jewish communal causes ("giving").

While each of these attitudinal topics is subsumed primarily under one of the five headings, there is a significant degree of interplay among the headings, as ethnicity is a complex whole which cannot be neatly divided into its component parts.

Two preliminary operations were carried out on the data. First, a joint measure of current Jewish density was derived from the crosstabulation of the two Jewish density variables.[2] Second, a factor analysis was carried out on a large number of attitudinal measures. Clusters of variables bearing on central dimensions of ethnicity were chosen for presentation.

II. Associations of Attitudes and Jewish Density

A. Particularism

The cluster of variables which was labeled "Particularism" is presented in Table 5.1, together with the loading of each variable on this factor.

Table 5.1: Particularism

	factor loading
1. reaction to community becoming all Jewish suburb	.76
2. desired community composition: proportion of Jews	.65
3. proportion of friends of an American Jew should be Jewish	.60
4. importance that most of children's friends be Jewish	.55
5. attitude towards Jewish day schools in America	.50

Both variables relating to community composition were highly associated with Jewish density (Table 5.2). While fewer than four in ten respondents in the high Jewish density category would react negatively to their community becoming an all Jewish suburb, almost eight in ten of those in the low Jewish density category would react negatively to such a development. No one in the high Jewish density group would opt for a community which consists of only "some or few" Jews. No one in the low Jewish density category prefers an "all or most(ly)" Jewish community, and over 70% would opt for a community with only "some or few" Jews. Within the components of the Jewish density variable, reaction to the prospect of the community becoming all Jewish was more highly associated with the proportion of Jews in the respondent's present community.

The respondents' overwhelming preference is for a replication of their current community situation. Over 85% of those currently living in a community perceived as all or mostly Jewish, over 95% of those living in

Table 5.2: Desired Community Composition BY
Jewish Density

Reaction to Community Becoming All Jewish Suburb	Jewish Density			
	high	mixed	low	
positive or no difference	62.8	31.6	20.8	
negative	37.2	68.4	79.2	
column	86	98	48	232
totals	37.1	42.2	20.7	100%

gamma 0.55

Proportion Jewish Want Community	Jewish Density			
	high	mixed	low	
all or most	48.8	7.1	0.0	
around half	51.2	38.4	27.1	
some or few	0.0	54.5	72.9	
column	86	99	48	233
totals	36.9	42.5	20.6	100%

gamma 0.84

a community perceived as half Jewish, and over 70% of the respondents who live in a community perceived as having only some or few other Jews would want their current situation replicated.

Whether this represents the *effect* of residential concentration on *attitudes towards* residential concentration or is a function of self-selection wherein the ethnic factor serves as a consideration in choosing among otherwise equally attractive areas of residence is a question best addressed by longitudinal data. It is clear, however, that Jewish density and more particularly the Jewish composition of the respondent's current community are positively associated with attitudes towards community composition.

The "friends" component of the Particularism factor consists of two parts. The first concerns the general attitude about what proportion of the friends of an American Jew should be Jewish; the second, attitudes about the Jewish friendship patterns of one's children. As could be expected based on previous discussion, a stronger association was found between Jewish density and the children's friendship variable than between Jewish density and the generalized attitude towards associational concentration. That is, the discrepancy between behavior and attitude in the matter of friendship patterns is reduced when the concern is with the friendship of children.

Both of the attitudinal measures concerning associational concentration were positively associated with Jewish density. Whereas 65.1% of the high Jewish density group express the opinion that at least half of an American Jew's friendship network should consist of other Jews, only 27.1% of the low Jewish density group express a similar attitude (Table 5.3). Approximately three of every ten respondents in both groups feel that the Jewish composition of one's friendship circle doesn't matter. However, while only one-quarter of the high Jewish density respondents also feel that it is unimportant that their children have mostly Jewish friends, over 60% of the low Jewish density respondents feel likewise.[3] Thus current Jewish density is also positively associated with attitudes towards associational concentration.

The final component of the Particularism factor is the attitude towards

Table 5.3: Attitudes towards Friendship
Patterns BY Jewish Density

Proportion Friends of American Jew Should Be Jewish	Jewish Density			
	high	mixed	low	
most	38.8	15.5	6.3	
about half	26.3	22.7	20.8	
some or few	6.3	27.8	41.7	
doesn't matter	28.8	34.0	31.3	
column	80	97	48	225
totals	35.6	43.1	21.3	100%

gamma 0.25

How Important Children's Friends Be Jewish	Jewish Density			
	high	mixed	low	
important	75.6	50.5	37.5	
unimportant	24.4	49.5	62.5	
column	86	99	48	233
totals	36.9	42.5	20.6	100%

gamma 0.48

Jewish day schools in America. In this instance, the association with Jewish density was weaker than that of the other Particularism factor variables. The widespread Jewish antipathy to parochial education as somewhat "un-American," an issue on which Jews have traditionally sided with Protestant opposition to Catholic advocacy, is apparently sufficient to lessen the effects of Jewish density.[4]

The relationship between the Particularism factor variables and Jewish density highlights an important finding in relation to the central research questions of this study. Current Jewish density is positively associated with attitudes towards residential and associational concentration. Jewish density is positively associated with one of the major components of Jewish ethnicity, the distinction between Jews and others.

B. Group Belonging and Identification

The second cluster of variables to emerge from the factor analysis of attitudinal measures is presented in Table 5.4.

Table 5.4: Group Belonging and Identification

	factor loading
1. identification	.70
2. good Jewish education: strengthening commitment to the Jewish people	.66
3. survival	.58
4. in-group feelings	.53

A strong association was found between the measure of "identification with the Jewish group"[5] and Jewish density (Table 5.5). Twice as many respondents in the high density category as in the low density category are to be found in the high identification group. Among the components of the Jewish density measure, the element of associational concentration contributes more strongly to this relationship.

Respondents were asked to rate a series of items as to their importance in a good Jewish education. The item "strengthening commitment

Table 5.5: Identification BY Jewish Density

	Jewish Density			
	high	mixed	low	
high identification	52.3	45.8	26.1	
medium/low identif.	47.7	54.2	73.9	
column	86	96	46	228
totals	37.7	42.1	20.2	100%
gamma 0.30				

to the Jewish people," was positively associated with Jewish density. Once again it was the associational component which contributed more strongly to the overall relationship.

The "survivalist" measure is derived from the summary of three of the "good Jew" items, each of which "constitute activities and attitudes ordinarily thought of as characteristic of 'survivalist' Jews."[6] These items relate to three of the most basic elements perceived as necessary for the continued survival of the Jewish group: Israel, the national homeland and a major source of contemporary Jewish identification; the synagogue, the primary local institutional expression of the Jewish community; and endogamous marriage, perceived as the sine qua non of continued group existence.

The relationship between survivalism and Jewish density, though positive, is weak. Approximately two-thirds of all respondents endorse at least the desirability of each of these elements of Jewish survival.[7] Among the Jewish density measures, it is once again – as is true for all of the components of this factor – the element of friendship patterns which is most strongly related to the survivalist impulse.

Finally, a scale of attitudinal measures was constructed based on responses to fourteen items which relate to in-group feelings. These included items on residential and associational concentration, identification, intermarriage, philanthropy, reasons for celebration of Jewish observances, and hopes for the Jewishness of one's children. The correlation

between in-group feelings and Jewish density was strong, with the associational concentration component again the major contributing factor.
Approximately one-half of those in the high density group, one-third of
those in the mixed density group, and one-sixth of those in the low density group are in the high in-group feelings category (Table 5.6). More
than twice as many of those in the low as opposed to the high Jewish
friendship group are in the low in-group feelings category.

Table 5.6: In-Group Feelings BY Jewish Density

In-Grp Feelings	Jewish Density			
	high	mixed	low	
high	48.8	33.7	16.7	
medium	34.9	39.6	25.0	
low	16.3	26.7	58.3	
column	86	101	48	235
totals	36.6	43.0	20.4	100%

gamma 0.43

Jewish density and especially the proportion of Jews among the respondent's friends are thus positively associated with group belonging and
identification. High Jewish density is shown once again to be related to
more positive Jewish attitudes on a central dimension of Jewish ethnicity.

C. Hopes and Expectations for Children

The two items which clustered on this factor are listed in Table 5.7.

Table 5.7: Hopes and Expectations for Children

	factor loading
1. how Jewish you would like your children to be ("hopes")	.84
2. how Jewish you think your children will actually be ("expectations")	.83

Only the associational concentration element of Jewish density bears a positive relationship with this factor, and that relationship was rather weak.

There is virtually no difference in expectations for the Jewishness of one's children between those with more and those with less Jewish friendship patterns. Those with more Jewish friends tend to have somewhat higher hopes for the Jewishness of their children. The lack of difference in expectations despite higher hopes bespeaks the respondents' perception of the ineffectiveness of Jewish associational concentration as an influence on the Jewishness of children. Coupled with the fact that nearly half of the total sample has high hopes for the Jewishness of their children while only one-quarter has high expectations, this would seem to indicate a perception of powerlessness to counteract the leveling influence of the general culture in which the respondents and their children are so thoroughly immersed.

D. Israel

Four questionnaire items on Israel loaded highly on this factor. They are presented in Table 5.8.

Table 5.8: Israel

	factor loading
1. How important is it that Israel be: a spiritual homeland for the Jewish people	.79
2. To what extent do you agree that the existence of Israel is essential for the continuation of American Jewish life	.73
3. How important is it that Israel be: a world center for Jewish culture	.63
4. How important in a good Jewish education is: developing a strong feeling for Israel	.51

Only on the residential concentration dimension of Jewish density did clear and consistent differences emerge. More of those in the more Jewish community category consider it very important that Israel be both a spiritual homeland and a center for Jewish culture (Table 5.9).

Two additional questions were asked regarding the role of Israel which did not load highly on the Israel factor. The first of these was "How important is it that Israel be: a place of refuge for Jews in distress?"; the second, "How important is it that Israel be: a potential place of refuge for American Jews?" In each case more of those in the more Jewish communities stress the importance of these potential roles for Israel (Table 5.9).

We note that Israel is perceived first and foremost as a place of refuge for Jews in distress. This function is accepted by the overwhelming majority of respondents regardless of their place in the Jewish density scheme. This is in accordance with what is generally known about the Zionism of American Jews: despite deep and broad support for Israel among American Jews, Zionism is for them largely a vicarious experience. That is, Israel must exist and be supported in its struggle for existence; Israel even plays an important role in the Jewish identity of American Jews; but ultimately it is for "them", for Jews other than those living in America who need it as a safe refuge.

To confirm this perception we need only take note of the fact that the role of Israel as a potential place of refuge for American Jews places last among the four potential roles which Israel might fulfill. Second among Israel's potential roles is the religious function of spiritual homeland. Functioning as a center for Jewish culture is important but less so. In America, after all, Jews are defined and define themselves – publicly at least – primarily as a religious group.

Given these conceptions of the role of Israel, how did the respondents react to the statement that "the existence of Israel is essential for the continuation of American Jewish life?" The majority of respondents clearly agree (Table 5.10). There is, however, a difference according to community composition. While 81.6% of those in communities which are half or more Jewish agree or strongly agree with this statement, only

Table 5.9: Importance of Roles of Israel BY
Proportion of Jews in the Community

	Proportion of Jews in Community		
	half or more	some or few	
Spiritual Homeland			
very important	70.0	60.3	
less important	30.0	39.7	
column	110	126	236
totals	46.6	53.4	100%
gamma 0.21			
Center Jewish Culture			
very important	60.9	43.7	
less important	39.1	56.3	
column	110	126	236
totals	46.6	53.4	100%
gamma 0.33			
Refuge Jews in Distress			
very important	83.5	77.8	
less important	16.5	22.2	
column	109	126	235
totals	46.4	53.6	100%
gamma 0.18			
Refuge American Jews			
very important	55.7	41.9	
less important	44.3	58.1	
column	106	124	230
totals	46.1	53.9	100%
gamma 0.27			

67.2% of those in communities having only some or few Jews do likewise.

Table 5.10: Extent Agree Existence of Israel
Essential for American Jewish Life
BY Proportion of Jews in Community

	half or more	some or few	
strongly agree	48.6	36.1	
agree	33.0	31.1	
disagree	18.3	32.8	
column	109	122	231
totals	47.2	52.8	100%
gamma 0.27			

Finally, what of the importance of developing a strong feeling for Israel as a component in a good Jewish education? Again, while there is general agreement about its importance, differences of degree do show up according to residential concentration. The consistent pattern in the association between residential concentration and the Israel variables holds: more of those in the more Jewish community settings feel that it is very important to develop a strong feeling for Israel.

While differences in attitudes about Israel are not highly related to differences in friendship patterns, they are strongly associated with differences in residential concentration. Jewish residential clustering is thus associated with more positive Jewish attitudes regarding the role and importance of Israel, a major focal point of contemporary Jewish identity and one of the central components of the common content shared by American Jews.

E. Intermarriage

The issue of intermarriage has been a point of critical concern to American Jews. Accurate estimates of the current and cumulative rates of intermarriage are difficult to ascertain; intermarried couples are generally underrepresented in surveys of American Jews. There are, according to the best estimates available, wide variations in the rate of intermarriage in different geographical areas where the proportion of Jews in the respective local populations varies greatly.

What does seem clear from some empirical and much anecdotal evidence is that the rate of intermarriage has been and is rising. This has been a major cause of alarm in the American Jewish community as continued endogamy is perceived as a necessary condition for the survival of American Jewry. Even those who are not so alarmed by the intermarriage rate per se are less sanguine about the effects of intermarriage on the quality of American Jewish life.

Respondents were asked to choose from among a variety of alternatives expressing how they would *feel* if a child of theirs were to consider marrying a non-Jew and what they would most likely *do* in the same situation.[8] While over 90% of the total sample would feel negatively about the prospect of their child marrying a non-Jew, just over 60% would act to oppose or discourage such an intermarriage and only a bit over 10% would "strongly oppose" it. In light of the overwhelming percentage of respondents with negative feelings about a prospective intermarriage, the lower percentage who would actively oppose it again suggests – as in the case of expectations for the Jewishness of one's children – that the respondents feel rather powerless to counteract the by-products of acculturation to, interaction with, and acceptance in the general society.

Although the prospective intermarriage would meet with some degree of negative feelings from the vast majority of respondents in all three Jewish density categories, there are clear differences in the strength of reaction (Table 5.11). While almost one-half of the high and mixed Jewish density categories would feel very negative, less than one- fifth of the low Jewish density group would feel likewise. While 71.5% of the high Jewish density respondents would strongly oppose or discourage such a prospective intermarriage, 63.4% of the mixed category, and only 40% of the low category would do likewise. Those in the higher Jewish density categories once again express more positive Jewish attitudes along a critical dimension of Jewish ethnicity.

The strongest associations were found between these intermarriage questions and the associational concentration component of Jewish density.

Table 5.11: Reactions to Intermarriage BY
Jewish Density

How Would You Feel	Jewish Density			
	high	mixed	low	
very negative	47.7	47.5	18.8	
somewhat negative	47.7	45.5	68.8	
no difference	4.7	6.9	12.5	
column	86	101	48	235
totals	36.6	43.0	20.4	100%

gamma 0.29

What Would You Do				
strongly oppose	15.5	10.9	6.7	
discourage	56.0	52.5	33.3	
be neutral	11.9	14.9	17.8	
accept	16.7	21.8	42.2	
column	84	101	45	230
totals	36.5	43.9	19.6	100%

gamma 0.30

Nearly twice as many respondents who report an all or mostly Jewish friendship network would feel very negative towards a prospective intermarriage and fewer than half as many of these same respondents would accept it.

With this general picture of response to intermarriage in mind, we turn to the intermarriage factor variables. The first results from an open-ended probe to the "how would you *feel*" section of the intermarriage question. The second is the "to transmit Jewishness to my children" response to a question probing the reasons behind celebration of Jewish holidays and observance of Jewish customs. The logical connection which complements the statistical association of these two variables is the common concern with the future Jewish status of one's children and the continuation of Jewishness through the next generation.

The open-ended responses were coded into the following three categories: 1) concern with the Jewish identity of one's children and with the continuation of Jewish tradition and the Jewish people; 2) feeling more comfortable with a Jewish son/daughter-in-law, "that's the way is should be," etc.; and 3) concern with difficulties in marriage arising from the mixed background of the intermarried couple. Though in some cases the differences are small, the consistent pattern is that the respondents in the *low* Jewish density categories (for the combined Jewish density measure and both its residential and associational parts) are more concerned with the threat to Judaism, in general or specifically as it affects their children. Respondents in the *higher* Jewish density categories dwell more on "Jewish comfort" and "difficulties in marriage."

Understanding these differences as differences in the manner in which concerns about intermarriage *are expressed* facilitates a plausible interpretation of this pattern.[9] In a situation of relatively lower Jewish density, the continuation of Jewish identity for one's children or the future of Judaism itself may be less taken for granted; the threats are more obvious. Concern is thus expressed along these lines. In a situation of relatively higher Jewish density, the "comfort" expression may be somewhat more prevalent as the more Jewish environment gives rise to expectations of Jewish consistency and continuity. In a situation of relatively higher Jewish density, where the future – both individual and collective – seems *relatively* more secure, concern is expressed not in terms of the Jewish future, but rather the way is left open for the "difficulties in marriage" argument to come to the fore.

This is a significant departure from the standard view which holds that it is the more acculturated Jews who feel compelled to voice their gut objection to intermarriage in terms that are palatable in the universalistic environment of suburban America, i.e., not the particularism of in-group concern but rather the universal problem of increasing marital disharmony.

In terms of citing transmission of Jewishness to one's children as a reason for Jewish celebration and observance, a small but consistent difference in emphasis emerges with the respondents in the higher Jewish density categories considering this a more important consideration than the respondents in the lower Jewish density categories.[10]

F. Anti-Semitism and Chosenness

The anti-Semitism and chosenness measures are presented together for two reasons. Statistically, each of these variables was associated in the factor analysis with one additional variable in common. Substantively, these two topics are obversely related. Anti-Semitism is a perception of out-group hostility toward the in-group; chosenness, of in-group particularity. Both are related to a central dimension of Jewish ethnicity, the distinction between Jews and others.

Those respondents living in more Jewish community settings perceive anti-Semitism as a more serious problem (Table 5.12).[11] One possible interpretation of this association would posit that those living in what are generally perceived as Jewish areas are more likely to experience anti-Semitic acts committed from the outside against their community. However, an opposing view – that those living in areas where Jews constitute a smaller proportion of the population are more likely to experience anti-Semitism from within their community – is also plausible. A likely explanation of this association may lie in different perceptions of the distinctions between Jews and non-Jews, which are associated with both Jewish residential concentration and perceptions of anti-Semitism.

Table 5.12: How Much of a Problem Is
Anti-Semitism in the United States
BY Proportion of Jews in Community

	half or more	some or few	
extremely serious	15.6	6.5	
fairly serious	45.9	34.7	
moderate	38.5	58.1	
not a problem	0.0	0.8	
column	109	124	233
totals	46.8	53.2	100%
gamma 0.38			

Turning to the concept of chosenness, respondents were asked: "In your opinion, are Jews the chosen people?" The idea of chosenness, even when intentionally left open to definition by the respondents themselves, is accepted by only one-third of the sample.

This traditional concept, despite attempts at redefinition in terms more acceptable to the universalistic American temper, retains too particularistic an ideological tone. It, like parochial education, suffers from the stigma of being somehow opposed to the basic fabric of America. Even among those who answered in the affirmative, over one-third sought to neutralize the particularistic impact of the concept by defining chosenness as implying a "mission, social responsibility, or compassion," or by claiming that in fact "all people are chosen."

There was virtually no difference in acceptance of chosenness according to categories of residential concentration and only slightly more of those reporting a higher proportion of Jewish friends accept the notion of chosenness.

G. Giving

The importance of *tzedakkah* [12] as a traditional Jewish value and its functional necessity in supporting the institutions and organizations of the Jewish community are well-known. Respondents were asked about

both the object of their philanthropic support and their perceptions as
to the nature and source of giving as a value. While 44.5% of the sample
felt that giving is an obligation – in accord with the traditional Jewish
view – another 38.7% felt it was desirable and 16.8% that it was merely
optional. No clear differences emerged in terms of the various dimensions
of Jewish density.

Respondents were further asked whether they thought that Jews should
give more to Jewish or more to general community causes, or the same to
both; and whether for them supporting worthy causes is more a Jewish
value, more an American value, or equally Jewish and American. Overall,
while 63.7% expressed the feeling that Jews should give more to Jewish
causes, almost an identical proportion (63.3%) felt that the value was
equally Jewish and American (Table 5.13).

Table 5.13: Giving: Recipient and Source of
Value

Do you think that Jews should give more to
Jewish or more to general community causes,
or the same to both?

more to Jewish	63.7
more to general	4.9
same to both	31.4
column	226
totals	100%

For *you*, is supporting worthy causes more a
Jewish value, more an American value, or
equally Jewish and American?

more a Jewish value	32.3
more an American value	4.4
equally Jewish & American	63.3
column	226
totals	100%

For purposes of analysis in terms of Jewish density, a combined measure
of these two giving dimensions was devised. A higher proportion of those

respondents in both the higher residential and associational categories felt that while giving was an equally Jewish and American value, Jews should give more to Jewish causes. Current Jewish density is positively related to the modal philanthropic category where giving is considered both a Jewish and American value, but Jews choose to give more to Jewish causes.

H. Camp

One additional attitudinal measure concerning children was tested for its relation to Jewish density. Once again, the striking nature of the concern with transmission of Jewishness to the next generation is evident. Respondents were asked a series of questions about the nature and content of a camp they would choose for their children. One such question was the following: "In choosing a camp for your child, how important would it be that the camp have...mostly Jewish campers and staff?"

While a majority of those who responded considered this (and all other Jewish camp content as well) unimportant,[13] significant differences do emerge in terms of Jewish density. Two-thirds of those in the high density group but only one-fourth of those in the low density group consider the Jewish composition of the camp important (Table 5.14).

Table 5.14: Camp: Mostly Jewish Campers and
Staff BY Jewish Density

	high	mixed	low	
important	66.7	41.5	24.4	
unimportant	33.3	58.5	75.6	
column	84	94	45	223
totals	37.7	42.2	20.2	100%
gamma 0.52				

There is thus a strong positive correlation between current Jewish density and preference for a Jewish camp setting in terms of other campers and staff being Jewish. A clear positive association once again emerges between Jewish density and attitudes connected to a central element of Jewish ethnicity, in this instance the element of group maintenance and continuity through the next generation.

I. Observance

One behavioral measure relating to a major component of the shared heritage of the group was included in the analysis by Jewish density. Observance of both Hanukkah and Passover in some fashion was nearly universal among the respondents,[14] and fully half of the sample also light candles on the Sabbath. Are there differences in these observances according to variations in Jewish density?

Those in the relatively *less* dense Jewish communities tend to observe slightly *more*, while those with relatively *more* Jewish friends tend to observe slightly *more*. It is thus friendship pattern rather than residential concentration that bears a positive relationship with this combined measure of Jewish observance.

III. Summary

What, then, is the composite picture which emerges from this analysis of the relationship between attitudes and Jewish density?

As can be seen from the summary statistical table (Table 5.15), the combined measure of Jewish density correlated positively with the Particularism factor including both its community and associational components, with aspects of the Group Belonging and Identification factor, with reaction to a prospective intermarriage, and with preference for a camp situation in which most of the campers and staff are Jewish.

The residential concentration dimension of Jewish density was most positively related to the community component of the Particularism factor. It was also positively associated with attitudes on the essentiality of Israel and the nature of Israel's role, with perceptions as to the seriousness of anti-Semitism in the United States, and with preference for a Jewish camp setting.

The associational concentration dimension of Jewish density bore the

Table 5.15: Summary Statistical Table
Attitudes and Jewish Density*

	Jewish Density gamma	Jews Commun. gamma	Jews Friends gamma
A. Particularism			
IF ALL JEWISH SUBURB	0.55	0.63	
% JEWISH WANT COMMUNITY	0.84	0.92	
% FRIENDS BE JEWISH	0.25		
IMPT KIDS' FRIENDS JEWISH	0.48		
FEEL ABOUT DAY SCHOOLS	0.17		
B. Group Belonging and Identification			
IDENTIFICATION	0.30	0.14	0.46
COMMITMENT JEWISH PEOPLE	0.16	0.09	0.23
SURVIVAL	0.12	0.06	0.19
IN-GROUP FEELINGS	0.43	0.37	0.46
C. Hopes and Expectations for Children			
HOPES			0.16
EXPECTATIONS			0.04
D. Israel			
SPIRITUAL HOMELAND		0.21	
CENTER JEWISH CULTURE		0.33	
REFUGE JEWS IN DISTRESS		0.18	
REFUGE AMERICAN JEWS		0.27	
ESSENTIAL AMERICAN JEWISH LIFE		0.27	
JEWISH ED: FEELING FOR ISRAEL		0.29	
E. Intermarriage			
FEEL ABOUT INTERMARRIAGE	0.29		0.49
DO ABOUT INTERMARRIAGE	0.30		0.33
REASONS NEGATIVE FEELINGS		-0.21	-0.10
TRANSMIT J'NESS CHILDREN	0.11	0.10	0.12
F. Anti-Semitism and Chosenness			
ANTI-SEMITISM IN U.S.		0.38	
ARE JEWS CHOSEN PEOPLE		0.12	
G. Giving			
SOURCE VALUE & RECIPIENT		-0.09	0.04
H. Camp			
JEWISH CAMPERS & STAFF	0.52	0.45	0.52
I. Observance			
HANUKKAH/PASSOVER/CANDLES		-0.12	0.27

*selected crosstabulations

strongest positive association with aspects of the Group Belonging and Identification factor, with reactions to intermarriage, and with the importance of the Jewish composition of a prospective camp. It also correlated positively with the observance of three widely celebrated Jewish occasions and to some extent with hopes for the Jewishness of one's children.

Comparison of the list associated with residential concentration and that associated with friendship composition prompts the following observation. Community composition seems to bear more on generalized attitudes that are somewhat more abstract than are those connected with associational concentration. The latter, by contrast, seem to be more immediate and personal, touching more on the content – and less on the framework – of life. This respective affinity of factors makes perfect sense: the community provides the framework or general environment in which family life is lived; friendships impinge rather more as a content with which that framework is intentionally filled.

Children and the importance attached to the transmission of identity to the next generation play a mediating role in increasing the legitimacy of particularism, especially in regard to the dimension of friendship patterns. We note the association of more Jewish friendship patterns with four elements involving children: hopes for the Jewishness of children, intermarriage, the Jewish composition of a camp community, and the observances of Hanukkah, Passover, and the lighting of Sabbath candles. In regard to the latter behavioral dimension, we remember that "to transmit Jewishness to my children" was the reason most cited behind observances and also figures as one of the central criteria affecting the selective retention of ritual among American Jews.[15]

Another theme which emerges from the analysis of attitudes and Jewish density is the rejection of that which is tainted with the aura of "un-American." Chosenness is rejected by two-thirds of the sample regardless of their situation in terms of Jewish density. Day schools, despite their potential contribution to the Jewishness of the next generation, are favored by less than one-fifth of the respondents.

In addition to noting the nature of response to the prospect of intermarriage and the positive correlation between reactions to intermarriage and associational concentration, we noted the particular pattern which characterizes expressions of concern about intermarriage for the various Jewish density categories. This pattern was seen to imply an interpretation different from that commonly put forth in the field.

The traditional concept of giving as an obligation was accepted by approximately two-fifths of the sample. Though a minority see it as a specifically Jewish value, a majority favor giving more to Jewish causes.

Finally, and perhaps most importantly, we note the *positive association of Jewish density with attitudes more supportive of central dimensions of Jewish ethnicity* across virtually all of the attitudinal areas tested.[16]

Notes

1. The observance measure is the one behavioral variable included in this list.

2. The new variable, labeled simply "Jewish Density," is defined as follows: "High" = proportion of Jews in the community: half or more, *and* proportion of Jews among friends: all or most; "Mixed" = proportion of Jews in the community: half or more, *and* proportion of Jews among friends: half or less *OR* proportion of Jews in the community: some or few, *and* proportion of Jews among friends: all or most; "Low" = proportion of Jews in the community: some or few, *and* proportion of Jews among friends: half or less.

3. Unlike the community composition dimension discussed above, no significant difference was found in the relation between the two components of the Jewish density variable and the associational composition dimension of particularism.

4. Nonetheless, while the modal response for each Jewish density category is "neither favor nor oppose," differences do emerge in the ratio of "favor" to "oppose" that distinguish the high Jewish density group from the mixed and low groups. While approximately equal proportions of the high Jewish density group "favor" and "oppose" day schools, nearly twice as many of the mixed and low density groups oppose as favor Jewish parochial education.

5. The measure of identification with the Jewish group is a summary scale designed from the extent to which the respondent expressed agreement with each of the following three items:

1. I feel closer to other Jews than to other Americans;

2. I feel a greater sense of responsibility to other Jews than to other Americans;

3. When I hear someone make a negative comment about Jews in general, I usually *do not* take any personal offense.

6. Sklare and Greenblum, op. cit., p. 327.

7. To be included in the "survivalist" category, a respondent had to have answered "essential" or "desirable" on each of the three items.

8. These questions are a replication of items asked in the 1975 Boston study. See Fowler, op. cit., pp. 66-70.

9. I am indebted to Calvin Goldscheider for this clarification. In his own analysis of similar data from the 1975 Boston study, he found that the common concern was the same – simply an underlying concern with intermarriage. Differences were rather variations in how that concern was expressed.

10. In the focus on comparing the Jewish density categories, we should not lose sight of the fact that the transmission of Jewishness to one's children was the reason most cited behind Jewish observance and celebration.

11. In addition to the relationship between perceptions of anti-Semitism and residential concentration, we note that just over 10% of the sample perceives anti-Semitism as an "extremely serious" problem in the United States, 40% a "fairly serious" problem, and half of the sample perceives it as only a "moderate" problem. Virtually no one, regardless of the Jewish composition of the community in which they live, feels that it is "not a problem at all."

12. The traditional Jewish term *tzedakkah*, has a nuance far different from "charity." *Tzedakkah* stems from the Hebrew root meaning "justice," and giving is perceived not as an optional act of kindness, but rather as a social obligation.

13. In fact, the positive response to this aspect of the Jewishness of the hypothetical camp was higher than that for any of the other Jewish aspects which included Sabbath services, classes in Jewish religion or in Jewish history and culture, and kosher food.

14. Only 1.7% "never" observe Hanukkah, while 78.6% "always" do; only 0.08% "never" observe Passover, while 83.6% "always" do.

15. For a discussion of the criteria which favor or mitigate against the retention of a particular ritual or celebration, see Marshall Sklare, *America's Jews*, pp. 110-117.

16. This chapter began with a statement that Jewish density would be treated as an independent variable and the attitudinal measures as dependent variables. As was taken into account, however, in the analytic scheme which underpins this research, given the unspecified nature of the time sequence involved, the implied causal sequence might just as well be reversed. Those associations which were discussed as significant in the framework of the effect of Jewish density on attitudes also emerge as significant relationships when analyzed in terms of the effects of attitudes on Jewish density.

Within the limitations of a cross-sectional study we are obliged in this regard (as opposed to the analysis of attitudes and background where the time sequence involved is clear and admits of causality in only one possible direction) to remain open to the plausibility of both interpretations. The investigation may, for analytic purposes, be posed in the language of either or both causal sequences, but in the end we must remember that we are dealing with associations and not causal relationships.

CHAPTER SIX

THE RELATION BETWEEN ATTITUDES AND
GENERAL BACKGROUND

I. Association of Attitudes and General Background

A. Particularism

The youngest age group (30-39) most favored Jewish residential concentration. Whereas over half of those aged 30-39 would react positively
or at least neutrally to their community becoming an all Jewish suburb,
less than 40% of those aged 50-59 would have the same reaction. Almost
70% of the youngest age cohort express preference for a majority Jewish
community; the same is true of only 46.7% of the oldest age group (Table 6.1). It was also the youngest age group that currently lives in the
predominantly Jewish settings.

Table 6.1: Attitudes towards Residential
Concentration BY Age

Proportion Jewish Want Community	50-59	40-49	30-39	
half or more	46.7	62.4	69.6	
some or few	53.3	37.6	30.4	
column	45	125	56	226
totals	19.9	55.3	24.8	100%
gamma -0.27				

As a slight positive association was found between age and education (the
older the respondent, the higher the level of educational attainment) and
an inverse relationship between education and attitudes favoring Jewish
residential concentration, the preference of the younger respondents for
more Jewish residential settings may be mediated through the intervening variable of educational attainment.

Examination of the friendship aspect of particularism revealed relationships weaker than and different from those of age and the community aspect of particularism. It is the oldest age group, which also reported having the most Jewish friends, that most favored Jewish friendship patterns. Nonetheless, approximately one-third of all age groups claimed that the proportion of friends Jewish "doesn't matter" and a minority in all cases expressed the opinion that most of the friends of an American Jew should be Jewish. In terms of the friendship pattern of children, it was the middle age cohort that most expressed support for Jewish associational concentration.

Two things should be noted. The first is the contrast discussed previously between feelings towards friendship patterns in the abstract versus specifically in relation to one's children. In the latter case, over one-half of the sample expresses the importance that "most of your children's friends be Jewish," whereas only twenty percent of the sample feels that most of the friends of an American Jew should be Jewish. Second, it is the middle age group, that with the most children between the ages of eleven and eighteen, that most favors Jewish friends for their children.

No significant differences among the three age groups emerged in attitudes towards Jewish day schools.

Generation was found to correlate only with the importance of children's friends being Jewish. The first and second generations expressed the importance of homogeneous Jewish friendship networks for children more than the third and fourth generations. There was virtually no difference between the first and second generations as compared with the third and fourth generations on the other measures of particularism.

Educational attainment was inversely associated with attitudes towards both residential and associational concentration. While over half of those with a college degree or less would react positively or neutrally to the prospect of their community becoming an all Jewish suburb, the same attitude was expressed by only 30.2% of those with at least some graduate education. Whereas only half of the higher education group want a majority Jewish community, over three-fourths of the lower education group state this preference (Table 6.2).

Table 6.2: Attitudes towards Residential
Concentration BY Education

React If Become All Jewish	h.s. or less thru college	some grad thru grad/prof degree	
positively or no difference	54.3	30.2	
negatively	45.7	69.8	
column	105	126	231
totals	45.5	54.5	100%
gamma 0.47			

Proportion Jewish Want Community			
half or more	78.8	49.6	
some or few	21.2	50.4	
column	104	127	231
totals	45.0	55.0	100%
gamma 0.58			

One-third of the lower education group but only 12.1% of the higher education group express the opinion that an American Jew should have mostly Jewish friends; less than half of the higher education group but over 70% of the lower education group feel it is very important that most of their children's friends be Jewish (Table 6.3).

Table 6.3: Attitudes towards Associational
Concentration BY Education

Proportion Friends Should Be Jewish	h.s. or less thru college	some grad thru grad/prof degree	
most	33.7	12.1	
half or fewer	39.6	51.6	
doesn't matter	26.7	36.3	
column	101	124	225
totals	44.9	55.1	100%
gamma 0.34			

How Important Kids Friends Be Jewish			
important	70.5	46.9	
unimportant	29.5	53.1	
column	105	128	233
totals	45.1	54.9	100%
gamma 0.46			

Thus on each measure of residential and associational concentration, over 20% more of those in the lower educational attainment category favor the more particularistic response.[1] Secular education once again proves to be a potentially significant intervening variable, with higher levels of educational attainment associated with more universalistic attitudes.

Those with relatively more education both favored and opposed Jewish day schools more than those with relatively less education. In other words, a higher proportion of the latter "don't feel strongly one way or the other."[2]

As with educational attainment, a uniform pattern emerged in the relationship between the residential and associational Particularism variables and occupational prestige. Housewives gave the most Jewish responses, followed by those in the relatively lower occupational prestige category. In all cases, those with relatively higher occupational prestige expressed the least Jewish attitudes. Overall on these measures (Table 6.4), the larger differences are between housewives and those in the labor force,[3] though there are also differences between the high and low prestige groups. No significant differences were found between occupational prestige categories and attitudes towards Jewish day schools.

Once again, the income measure is that of the *household* income (respondent and, if applicable, spouse) and not necessarily that of the respondent alone. A pattern similar to that of education and occupation emerged. In general, lower income was associated with more Jewish responses, though differences between income categories were relatively small.

No clear pattern emerged in the relationship between income and attitudes towards day schools. The low correlation between attitudes towards day schools and education, occupation, and income again reflects the general aversion among this population to day school education.

B. Group Belonging and Identification

No clear pattern of correlation emerged from the analysis of the Group Belonging and Identification variables by either age or generation. A moderate correlation exists between a relatively lower level of educational attainment and more positive Jewish responses on the "survivalist" and "in-group feelings" variables.

Relatively lower occupational prestige was similarly associated with more Jewish responses on the Group Belonging and Identification variables. Housewives were the most strongly identified with the Jewish group, followed by the lower occupational prestige category. In terms of both the "survival" variable and the scale of in-group feelings (Table 6.5), the distinction is clearly between housewives and those in the labor force.[4]

Table 6.4: Attitudes towards Residential and
Associational Concentration BY
Occupational Prestige

React If Become All Jewish Suburb	Occupational Prestige			
	housewives	low	high	
positively or no difference	63.0	41.2	31.1	
negatively	37.0	58.8	68.9	
column	27	136	61	224
totals	12.1	60.7	27.2	100%
gamma 0.32				

Proportion Jewish Want Community				
half or more	77.8	61.0	57.4	
some or few	22.2	39.0	42.6	
column	27	136	61	224
totals	12.1	60.7	27.2	100%
gamma 0.20				

How Important Kids Friends Be Jewish				
important	71.4	58.0	48.3	
unimportant	28.6	42.0	51.7	
column	28	138	60	226
totals	12.4	61.1	26.5	100%
gamma 0.25				

Table 6.5: Group Belonging and Identification
BY Occupational Prestige

Survival	housewives	low	high	
survival yes	85.7	65.7	65.6	
survival no	14.3	34.3	34.4	
column	28	137	61	226
totals	12.4	60.6	27.0	100%
gamma 0.19				
In-Group Feelings				
high	60.7	36.7	24.6	
medium	32.1	33.8	37.7	
low	7.1	29.5	37.7	
column	28	139	61	228
totals	12.3	61.0	26.8	100%
gamma 0.33				

No clear pattern emerged in the relationship between the Group Belonging and Identification variables and income.

C. Hopes and Expectations for Children

The only difference to emerge in terms of age groupings was that fewer of the oldest age group have high expectations for the Jewishness of their children. This may be due to the fact that the children of this age cohort are older and the actual level of their Jewishness is therefore more evident. Expectations held by this group are thus likely tempered to a greater extent by reality.

More of the housewives and lower occupational category had higher expectations for the Jewishness of their children (Table 6.6). This is in keeping with previous findings on the more Jewish patterns of housewives and those located towards the relatively lower end of the occupational prestige spectrum.

In terms of income categories, no differences were found in regard to

Table 6.6: Expectations for Jewishness of
Children BY Occupational Prestige

	Occupational Prestige			
Expectations	housewives	low	high	
high	32.1	29.0	17.2	
low	67.9	71.0	82.8	
column	28	131	58	217
totals	12.9	60.4	26.7	100%
gamma 0.25				

hopes, and the pattern was mixed in regard to expectations. Jewish factors played the largest role in interaction with Jewish friends for the lowest income category.

D. Israel

The oldest age group and the first and second generation see Israel more as a spiritual homeland, and less as a potential place of refuge for American Jews. A slightly higher proportion of the youngest age cohort and of the third and fourth generations stress that "the existence of Israel is essential for the continuation of American Jewish life."

These findings point to a different nuance in the role which Israel plays for the respective age groups. The older group better fits the more classic pattern among American Jews: the association with Israel is primarily through Judaism as a religion and Zionism is more thoroughly a vicarious experience. The younger group experiences Israel less specifically through religious associations and more as a central component of its identity, perhaps because their ties to Israel as young adults were established primarily in the period of the Six Day and Yom Kippur Wars.

A consistent pattern emerged across all three Israel measures in the analysis by educational attainment categories. More of those in the lower educational category express stronger positive responses (Table 6.7).[5] A similarly consistent pattern emerged from the analysis of the Israel

Table 6.7: Attitudes towards Israel BY
Education

How Important Israel: Spiritual Homeland	h.s. or less thru college	some grad thru grad/prof degree	
very important	72.6	57.4	
less important	27.4	42.6	
column	106	129	235
totals	45.1	54.9	100%
gamma 0.33			

How Important Israel: Refuge American Jews			
very important	56.3	42.1	
less important	43.7	57.9	
column	103	126	229
totals	45.0	55.0	100%
gamma 0.28			

To What Extent Agree: Existence of Israel Essential for American Jewish Life			
strongly agree	57.3	31.5	
agree	25.2	36.2	
disagree	17.5	32.3	
column	103	127	230
totals	44.8	55.2	100%
gamma 0.41			

variables and categories of occupational prestige. In each case, the highest percentage of positive responses was found in the housewives category and lowest among those with high occupational prestige.[6] While there is also a slight positive association between low income and a high percentage of positive response on the Israel variables, the pattern was less decisive than in the cases of educational attainment and occupational prestige.

Relatively lower educational attainment, occupational prestige, and to a lesser extent income were once again associated with a stronger Jewish response.

E. Intermarriage

The relationship between attitudes towards the Intermarriage variables and age reflects the heightened concerns of parents appropriate to the age of their children. As it was the 40-49 year-old group that most favored Jewish friends for their children, similarly a higher percentage of this middle age cohort, which has the most children at the age when dating is an issue, reacts negatively to the prospect of intermarriage. It is the youngest age group, which has the most children at the age when parents begin to be concerned about transmission of identity (and the age when parents start their children in Jewish education), that most considers transmission of Jewishness to one's children a very important reason for Jewish celebration and observance.

Findings by generation are similarly consistent. While more of the first and second generations would react negatively to a prospective intermarriage, slightly more of the third and fourth generations express the importance of the transmission of Jewishness as a motivation behind observance and celebration.

It is those in the lower categories of secular education, and housewives and those in the lower occupational prestige category who would react more negatively to a prospective intermarriage. Once again, lower levels of secular education and occupational prestige are associated with more positive responses along a dimension critically related to Jewish ethnicity. No significant differences were found in reaction to intermarriage in terms of analysis by income categories.

F. Anti-Semitism and Chosenness

Anti-Semitism in the United States was considered a more serious problem by respondents who are in the youngest age cohort and third or fourth generation. A similar position was held by those in the lower category of educational attainment, and by housewives and those in the lower occupational prestige category (Table 6.8). Only one respondent considered it not a problem at all.

The younger the age group, the higher the percentage of those who agreed that Jews are the chosen people (Table 6.9). More of the housewives and lower occupational category also expressed agreement. No differences were found in terms of generation and education. It is the lowest income category which most accepts the notion of chosenness, though the relationship between chosenness and income is not linear.

Table 6.8: How Much of a Problem Is
Anti-Semitism in the United States
BY Education, Occupational Prestige

	Education		
Anti-Semitism	h.s. or less thru college	some grad thru grad/prof degree	
serious	68.3	35.9	
moderate	31.7	64.1	
column	104	128	232
totals	44.8	55.2	100%
gamma 0.59			

	Occupational Prestige			
	housewives	low	high	
serious	70.4	50.0	42.6	
moderate	29.6	50.0	57.4	
column	27	138	61	226
totals	11.9	61.1	27.0	100%
gamma 0.26				

Attitudes towards both chosenness and the seriousness of anti-Semitism

Table 6.9: Are Jews the Chosen People BY Age

	50–59	40–40	30–39	
yes	23.8	31.9	45.1	
no	76.2	68.1	54.9	
column	42	116	51	209
totals	20.1	55.5	24.4	100%
gamma -0.28				

are related to perceptions of the distinction between Jews and others. As has proven to be consistently the case, relatively lower socioeconomic status is once again associated with more particularistic Jewish attitudes.

G. Giving

Those who expressed the opinion that giving was more a Jewish value and that Jews should give more to Jewish causes were younger, in the higher category of educational attainment,[7] and more affluent. While there was no difference between the higher and lower categories of occupational prestige, more housewives chose the "Jewish – Jewish" response.

Those who felt that giving was an equally Jewish and American value but that Jews should give more to Jewish causes were older, in the lower category of educational attainment, and in the lower income categories. A slightly higher percentage of those in the higher occupational prestige category also expressed this combination of attitudes, followed by housewives.

Examination of the distribution *within* each social characteristic category reveals the following. While "Jewish value - Jewish giving" is the modal response for the youngest age group and for the highest income category; and "equal value - Jewish giving" the modal response for the older age categories, the lower educational category, and the lower income categories; the "equal value - equal giving" response is not the modal response for any category of any of the social characteristics. Across all age cohorts and educational, occupational, and income categories, there is no group within the sample – regardless of whether or not they consider giving primarily a Jewish value – which can be characterized as in favor of supporting Jewish and general causes in equal measure.

Like the issue of Jewish friends for one's children, attitudes which are perceived as essential for Jewish survival are less easily modified by the counter-pressure of American egalitarian norms. The general emphasis on Jewish giving as a necessary foundation for the maintenance of Jewish communal organizations and institutions, and through them of the American Jewish community itself, appears for the present to have succeeded in withstanding this pressure.

H. Camp

Fewer in the older age cohort than in the younger groups felt it important that a prospective camp for their children have mostly Jewish campers and staff. This may be another example of age-specific or stage in the life-cycle concerns as the children of the older age cohort are generally beyond camp age.

A Jewish camp setting was favored by more of those in the lower educational category and more by housewives and those in the lower occupational prestige category (Table 6.10). Differences in terms of income were insignificant. Once again, lower levels of secular education and occupational prestige are positively associated with attitudes more supportive of group maintenance and continuity.

I. Observance

In terms of the one behavioral variable tested – the combined measure for the observance of Hanukkah, Passover, and the lighting of Sabbath candles – high observance was more typical of those in the high educational category, as well as of those in the labor force as opposed to housewives. The observance measure thus seems to be an exception to the general pattern of association between high education and occupation and less Jewish responses. As was also the case in the previous analysis of observance according to categories of residential concentration, high observance is associated with measures that are otherwise

Table 6.10: Camp: Mostly Jewish Campers and
Staff BY Education, Occupational
Prestige

	Education		
	h.s. or less thru college	some grad thru grad/prof degree	
important	60.6	38.7	
unimportant	39.4	61.3	
column	99	124	233
totals	44.4	55.6	100%

gamma 0.42

	Occupational Prestige			
	housewives	low	high	
important	63.0	49.6	35.6	
unimportant	37.0	50.4	64.4	
column	27	131	59	217
totals	12.4	60.4	27.2	100%

gamma 0.31

associated with less Jewish positions. This may reflect the attempt of parents who have not provided their children with particularly Jewish environments to nonetheless instill some sense of Jewish identity through the observance of child-centered ritual and celebration.

II. Summary

In light of trends among American Jews towards high levels of educational attainment, occupational prestige, and the entry of Jewish women into the labor force, the prognosis for the strength of attitudes favorable to the retention of the Jewish ethnic tie might appear less than favorable based on the preceding analysis.

Among the social characteristics tested, education and occupation were most strongly associated with attitudes towards residential concentration. Those in the lower educational and occupational categories most favor Jewish residential concentration.

Jewish associational concentration is also supported by more of those in the lower educational and occupational categories. In particular, attitudes in favor of residential and associational concentration are held by a lower percentage of those with at least some exposure to college and by a lower percentage of those in the labor force.

Identification with the Jewish group, attitudes favorable to Jewish survival, and in-group feelings are likewise held by more of those in the low educational and occupational groupings. Respondents in these same categories are more of the opinion that the existence of Israel is essential for American Jewish life, have higher expectations for the Jewishness of their children, and would choose a more Jewish camp environment for them.

There are, however, specific findings which mediate in favor of the persistence of Jewish ethnicity. For example, within the high occupational category, it is the free professions that least express the importance of Israel; movement among American Jews is now in the direction of the salaried professions. Further, the younger respondents and those in the high educational and occupational categories have by no means abandoned selected observances.

In terms of attitudes towards intermarriage, reactions were seen to be appropriate to the age of one's children. While more of the lower educational and occupational categories would react negatively to a prospective intermarriage, more of the younger respondents and of those in the high educational and occupational groupings saw transmission of Jewishness to their children as an important impetus to celebrate Jewish holidays and observe Jewish customs.

While anti-Semitism was seen as more of a problem in the United States by those in the low educational, occupational, and income categories, this same perception was held by more of the younger respondents. The idea of chosenness was similarly accepted by more of the younger respondents, though also supported by more of those in the lower occupational and income categories.

It was the youngest respondents and those in the high educational and high income categories who most chose the uniformly Jewish response regarding the value and object of giving. The uniformly general response ("equal value - equal giving") was the response least chosen by those in the high educational, high occupational, and high income categories.

The preceding analysis thus points to both positive and negative signs regarding the prospects for persistence of the Jewish ethnic tie. On the whole, however, in regard to the majority of the attitudinal variables tested, *high education*, and to a lesser extent high occupational status and high income, *is associated with relatively less Jewish attitudes*. It is therefore critical to be aware of education in particular and socioeconomic status in general as potentially significant intervening variables in the association among Jewish background, Jewish density, and attitudes.

Table 6.11: Summary Statistical Table
Attitudes and General Background*

	Age gamma	Gen. gamma	Ed. gamma	Occ. gamma	Inc. gamma
A. Particularism					
ALL JEWISH SUBURB	-0.16		0.47	0.32	0.14
% JEWISH WANT COMM	-0.27		0.58	0.20	0.18
% FRIENDS JEWISH	0.09		0.34	0.17	0.10
KIDS'FRNDS JEWISH	0.05	0.16	0.46	0.25	0.16
B. Group Belonging and Identification					
IDENTIFICATION				0.23	
SURVIVAL			0.14	0.19	
IN-GROUP FEELINGS			0.26	0.33	
C. Hopes and Expectations for Children					
HOPES				0.08	
EXPECTATIONS				0.25	
D. Israel					
SPIRITUAL HOMELAND			0.33	0.27	
REFUGE AMER. JEWS			0.28	0.27	
ESSENTIAL JEWISH LIFE			0.41	0.26	
E. Intermarriage					
DO RE INT'MARRIAGE	0.10				
J'NESS TO CHILDREN	-0.27				
F. Anti-Semitism and Chosenness					
ANTI-SEMITISM US	-0.22	-0.17	0.59	0.26	0.08
ARE JEWS CHOSEN	-0.28			0.18	0.11
G. Giving					
VALUE & RECIPIENT	0.04		-0.14	0.04	-0.19
H. Camp					
JEWISH CAMPERS & STAFF			0.42	0.31	

*selected crosstabulations

Notes

1. While the grouping of educational attainment levels presented in the crosstabulations was necessary in order to have a reasonable number of cases in the table cells, the sharpest division in terms of both residential and associational concentration was between those who never attended college and those with at least some exposure to college. The former were more in favor of both residential and associational concentration. This is suggestive given the long-standing trend among American Jews towards virtually universal college attendance.

2. In this instance, exposure to college was not a decisive factor.

3. The trend towards increased female employment may thus have an effect on Jewish attitudes as it has on the tradition of female involvement in American Jewish voluntary associations and communal institutions. In that regard, the entry of increasing numbers of Jewish women into the labor force has resulted in a decrease in the numbers available for volunteer service in these organizations and institutions and has threatened what formerly was in many cases the backbone of activity in these groups.

4. The question arises as to whether the higher percentage of housewives in the more Jewishly identified categories is due more to their occupational status (not being in the labor force) or more to their sex. To test for this, the same crosstabulations were run controlling for the sex of the respondent. No consistent pattern of male-female differences emerged. A similar control for sex was performed on the crosstabulations of the Particularism BY occupational prestige variables. Here once again the results were mixed.

5. In the analysis by more detailed categories of educational attainment, those in the "graduate or professional degree" component of the higher educational category expressed the least positive responses.

6. As in the case with education, it is the upper end of the high occupational prestige category that expressed the least positive responses.

7. The association of high educational attainment with a more Jewish response is discrepant with the generally observed universalistic impact of high levels of secular education. The explanation may lie in the role which giving has assumed for *some* American

Jews as a "painless" and token form of participation. For other American Jews, the explanation may be more in line with that presented at the end of this section on giving.

CHAPTER SEVEN

THE RELATION BETWEEN ATTITUDES AND JEWISH BACKGROUND

I. Associations of Attitudes and Jewish Background

A. Particularism

Of the three components of Jewish background, the residential and associational concentration of the respondent's early environment were most positively related to Particularism.

More than half of those who grew up in more Jewish communities would not react negatively to their current community becoming an all Jewish suburb, while less than one-fourth of those who grew up in less Jewish communities would do likewise (Table 7.1). In terms of ideal community composition, more than three-fourths of those who were raised in more Jewish communities would prefer a community where Jews constitute half or more of the population, while less than half of those who were raised in less Jewish communities express the same preference. Jewish background residential concentration is thus positively associated with attitudes towards preferred Jewish residential concentration.

Respondents whose parents identified as Reform were less likely than those whose parents identified as Orthodox or Conservative to favor Jewish residential concentration. The same is true of respondents who rated the observance of their parents as low compared with those who rated their parents' observance as high. An inverse relationship was found between the Jewish education of the respondent and the respondent's preference for Jewish residential concentration.

Attitudes towards Jewish associational concentration correlated most highly with the proportion of Jews among the respondent's childhood friends. Almost four times as many respondents who reported growing up with a majority of Jewish friends express the opinion that Jews should have mostly Jewish friends (Table 7.2). Jewish background associational concentration is thus positively associated with attitudes towards Jewish associational concentration.

Table 7.1: Attitudes towards Residential
Concentration BY Proportion of Jews
in Community Where Grew Up

React If Become All Jewish	Proportion of Jews Where Grew Up		
	half or more	some or none	
positively or no difference	53.8	23.3	
negatively	46.2	76.7	
column	130	103	233
totals	55.8	44.2	100%

gamma 0.59

Proportion Jewish Want Community			
half or more	77.9	41.2	
some or few	22.1	58.8	
column	131	102	233
totals	56.2	43.8	100%

gamma 0.67

Table 7.2: Proportion Friends Should Be Jewish
BY Proportion of Jews among
Childhood Friends

	Childhood Friends		
	all or most	half or fewer	
most	29.5	7.5	
half or fewer	39.0	58.8	
doesn't matter	31.5	33.8	
column	146	80	226
totals	64.6	35.4	100%

gamma 0.26

We note once again, however, that around one-third of the respondents regardless of their childhood friendship pattern say that the proportion of Jews among the friends of an American Jew "doesn't matter". Also striking is that only 29.5% of those who grew up with all or mostly Jewish friends express the opinion that most the friends of an American Jew should be Jewish. Despite the fact that approximately 70% of the respondents report actually having all or mostly Jewish friends and that approximately 65% report growing up with similar proportions of Jews among their friends, a mere 22% of the sample express the opinion that Jews should have mostly Jewish friends. Irrespective of their background and actual behavior, the attitude of the respondents towards friendship patterns on an ideal level, or at least that which they are willing to express, is clearly subject to the influence of the egalitarian and non-particularistic American norm.

A fairly strong correlation emerged between the importance to the respondents of a Jewish friendship network for their children and their own residential and associational patterns while growing up (Table 7.3). More than 60% of those who report growing up in majority Jewish communities and with all or mostly Jewish friends, but only a bit over 45% of those who report growing up in minority Jewish communities and with half or fewer Jewish friends feel that it is important that most of their children's friends be Jewish. Once again, the importance of a Jewish friendship network gains more support in relation to one's children than when posed in more general terms.

No strong or consistent correlation emerged in the relationship between Jewish background factors and the attitude towards Jewish day schools in America. The most consistent finding was that in the lower Jewish background categories there was generally a higher percentage of respondents who did not feel strongly about the subject of Jewish day schools one way or the other.

In terms of both specific attitudes towards residential and associational concentration and the overall thrust of the Particularism factor, more positive Jewish attitudes are expressed by those who report having grown up in situations of higher Jewish density. While there is also a positive association between attitudes on Particularism and selected aspects of

Table 7.3: How Important Children's Friends Be
Jewish BY Background Jewish Density

	Proportion Jews Community where Grew Up			Proportion Jews among Childhood Friends		
	half or more	some or none		all or most	half or fewer	
important	64.1	46.6		62.3	46.3	
unimportant	35.9	53.4		37.7	53.7	
column	131	103	234	154	82	236
totals	56.0	44.0	100%	65.3	34.7	100%
	gamma 0.34			gamma 0.31		

the Jewishness of the parental home, that relationship is weaker and less consistent. Jewish background, especially in terms of background Jewish density, is thus positively associated with more Jewish attitudes relating to the distinction between members of the group and others.

B. Group Belonging and Identification

More than twice as many respondents who grew up with relatively fewer Jewish friends are in the low category of identification with the Jewish group (Table 7.4). The relationship between identification and the proportion of Jews in the community where the respondent grew up was also positive, though less strong.

In terms of the survivalist variable (Israel, Synagogue, and Marriage items on the "good Jew" list), no difference was found between the categories of childhood residential concentration and only a slight difference between categories of childhood friendship patterns. While there was a positive relationship between survival and all of the variables measuring aspects of the Jewishness of the parental home, the relationship was in all cases weak.

The strongest positive association with the Jewish education measures

Table 7.4: Identification BY Proportion of
Jews among Childhood Friends

	Childhood Friends		
	all or most	half or fewer	
high	48.0	39.5	
medium	33.1	18.5	
low	18.9	42.0	
column	148	81	229
totals	64.6	35.4	100%
gamma 0.28			

was between survivalist attitudes and the actual Jewish education of the
respondent. While a majority of respondents in both Jewish education
categories hold survivalist attitudes, more of those in the high Jewish
education category do so.

The measure of in-group feelings was positively associated with both
childhood residential and associational concentration and with the Jewishness of the parental home in terms of items found or discussed there
(Table 7.5).

Table 7.5: In-Group Feelings BY Presence of
Jewish Objects, Discussion of
Jewish Topics in Parental Home

	Presence of Jewish Objects			Discussion of Jewish Topics		
	yes	no		yes	no	
high	47.8	32.5		48.0	26.6	
medium	32.6	36.1		34.7	36.0	
low	19.6	31.4		17.3	37.4	
column	46	191	237	98	139	237
totals	19.4	80.6	100%	41.4	58.6	100%
	gamma 0.28			gamma 0.41		

C. Hopes and Expectations for Children

The most striking finding in the relationship between hopes for the Jewishness of children and Jewish background was that there is almost no difference in the level of hopes for the various categories on almost all of the Jewish background factors. There was virtually no difference in terms of proportion of Jews in the community in which the respondent grew up and among childhood friends, nor among those respondents whose parents identified as Orthodox, Conservative, or Reform.

The strongest relationships were between hopes and the Jewish education variables. More of those in the high Jewish education category and more of those who considered their Jewish education a very important early influence on their current level of Jewishness had higher hopes for the Jewishness of their children.

In terms of expectations for the Jewishness of children, there was no difference according to the proportion of Jews in the childhood community or among childhood friends, or according to the self-definition or observance of parents. Further, on each of these variables, the percentage with high expectations was approximately one-half the percentage with high hopes. Differences did emerge when expectations were analyzed in terms of the remaining two measures of Jewishness in the parental home, with a higher percentage of those in whose parental homes Jewish objects were present and Jewish topics discussed having high expectations for the Jewishness of their children (Table 7.6).

A higher percentage of those who considered Jewish education a very important influence had high expectations for the Jewishness of their children.

While attitudes relating to this aspect of group maintenance are thus not associated with differences in background Jewish density, differences do emerge in terms of the Jewish content of the parental home and of the respondent's Jewish educational background.

D. Israel

More of those who reported growing up in more Jewish residential and

Table 7.6: Expectations for Children BY
Presence of Jewish Objects,
Discussion of Jewish Topics in
Parental Home

	Presence of Jewish Objects			Discussion of Jewish Topics		
	yes	no		yes	no	
high	34.1	23.5		34.4	19.1	
low	65.9	76.5		65.6	80.9	
column	44	183	227	96	131	227
totals	19.4	80.6	100%	42.3	57.7	100%
	gamma 0.25			gamma 0.38		

associational environments agreed strongly that the existence of Israel is essential for American Jewish life (Table 7.7).

More respondents from Orthodox than from Conservative homes and more from Conservative than from Reform homes felt that it was very important that Israel serve as "a spiritual homeland for the Jewish people." More respondents from Reform than from Conservative homes and more from Conservative than from Orthodox homes felt it was very important that Israel serve as "a potential place of refuge for American Jews".

This last finding is somewhat surprising in terms of the reputedly higher degree of attention paid by Reform Judaism to integration into the host environment. The combination of the two positions taken by those from Reform families is also striking in terms of the more "religious" and less "national" historic orientation of Reform Judaism.

This apparent paradox can perhaps be resolved by reference to the current status of the three Jewish "denominations" in Israel. While Orthodox Judaism is the official Judaism of Israel and Conservative Judaism is beginning to gain some recognition there (Conservative rabbis can, for

Table 7.7: What Extent Agree: Existence of
Israel Essential for American
Jewish Life BY Background Jewish
Density

	Community where Grew Up			Childhood Friends		
	half or more	some or none		all or most	half or fewer	
str. agree	45.0	38.8		49.7	30.0	
agree	34.1	29.1		27.2	40.0	
disagree	20.9	32.0		23.2	30.0	
column	129	103	232	151	80	231
totals	55.6	44.4	100%	65.4	34.6	100%
	gamma 0.17			gamma 0.28		

example, get ad hoc permission to perform marriages), Reform Judaism is uniformly held in low regard by the official Israeli religious establishment. This situation has been well publicized and affects the attitude of Reform Jews towards Israel's potential to serve as their "spiritual homeland."

There was a slight positive association between Jewish education and the extent to which respondents agreed that Israel is essential for American Jewish life. An inverse relationship was found between the Jewish education of the respondent and the importance of Israel as a potential refuge for American Jews.

Israel is a central focus of American Jewish identity and a major component of the shared heritage of American Jews. Attitudes towards the essentiality of Israel for American Jewish life, the issue which most directly addresses the centrality of Israel in American Jewish ethnicity, was the Israel variable most consistently related to Jewish background.

E. Intermarriage

Asked how they would feel about a prospective intermarriage involving their child, no differences emerged among the various categories of childhood residential or associational concentration or of Jewish education. Those from Reform homes would feel somewhat less negatively than those from Orthodox or Conservative homes. Slightly fewer respondents who rated the observance of their parental home as low would react negatively. The presence of Jewish objects and discussion of Jewish topics in the parental home were also weakly associated with negative reaction to a prospective intermarriage.

Asked what they would do in reaction to a prospective intermarriage, a slightly higher percentage of those in the higher childhood residential and friendship concentration categories responded that they would oppose or discourage it. Somewhat fewer of those from Reform than from Orthodox or Conservative homes would do likewise. More of those who rated their parents' observance as high and who remembered discussion of Jewish topics in their parental homes would oppose or discourage such a prospective intermarriage (Table 7.8).

The final variable related to intermarriage, the importance of transmission to children as a motivation for Jewish celebration and observance, was highly associated with the discussion of Jewish topics in the parental home (Table 7.9) and was also cited as very important by those who considered their early Jewish education an important influence.

Attitudes towards endogamy, perceived as a major element in group maintenance, are most consistently associated with aspects of the Jewishness of the parental home.

F. Anti-Semitism and Chosenness

More of those who rated the observance of their parents as high and of those who remember discussion of Jewish topics in their parental home considered anti-Semitism a more serious problem (Table 7.10).

Acceptance of the idea of chosenness was higher for those in the high Jewish education category, and for those who rated the observance of

Table 7.8: What Would You Do about a
Prospective Intermarriage BY
Observance of Respondent's
Parents, Discussion of Jewish
Topics in Parental Home

	Parental Observance		
	high	low	
oppose or discourage	66.4	52.4	
be neutral or accept	33.6	47.6	
column	131	105	236
totals	55.5	44.5	100%

gamma 0.29

	Discussion of Jewish Topics		
	yes	no	
oppose or discourage	70.1	52.9	
be neutral or accept	29.9	47.1	
column	97	138	235
totals	41.3	58.7	100%

gamma 0.35

Table 7.9: Reasons for Celebration: To
Transmit Jewishness to Children BY
Discussion of Jewish Topics in
Parental Home

	Discussion of Jewish Topics		
	yes	no	
very important	83.3	65.7	
less important	16.7	34.3	
column	96	137	233
totals	41.2	58.8	100%

gamma 0.45

Table 7.10: How Much of a Problem Is
Anti-Semitism in the United States
BY Observance of Respondent's
Parents, Discussion of Jewish
Topics in Parental Home

Observance of Respondent's Parents

	high	low	
serious	55.0	44.2	
moderate	45.0	55.8	
column	131	104	235
totals	55.7	44.3	100%

gamma 0.21

Discussion of Jewish
Topics in Parental Home

	yes	no	
serious	56.7	45.3	
moderate	43.3	54.7	
column	97	137	234
totals	41.5	58.5	100%

gamma 0.23

their parents as high and who remember the presence of Jewish objects in the home of their parents.

There was almost no difference in the acceptance of the chosenness concept among those from Orthodox, Conservative, or Reform homes. Despite the problematics of this concept in the American setting, this lack of difference is nonetheless interesting given the greater historic opposition of Reform Judaism to the notion of chosenness. Equal acceptance by those from Reform homes perhaps represents success in the effort by the Reform elite to redefine chosenness in terms of "mission."

In their drive to gain full participation in civil society and the concomitant impulse to minimize other than purely religious distinctions, the Reform elite were unable to accept the nuances traditionally associated with chosenness. They preferred instead to redefine the concept. They interpreted chosenness as bearing neither connotations of superiority nor of Jewish national identity, but rather that Jews had a mission to spread ethical social behavior – as exemplified in the prophetic writings – among the nations of the world in whose midst they were dispersed. This redefinition served the additional purpose of finding positive meaning in the dispersal, and thus reinforced claims of loyalty to their countries of citizenship and denials of hopes for the reconstitution of the Jewish nation in its own homeland.

G. Giving

The "Jewish value-Jewish giving" response was most highly associated with the discussion of Jewish topics in the respondent's parental home. Respondents from Reform homes chose this response more than respondents from Conservative homes; the latter chose this response more than respondents from Orthodox homes. The "equal value-Jewish giving" response was most positively associated with parental observance. There was no difference among those from Orthodox, Conservative, or Reform homes.

Those from Orthodox homes chose the "equal value-equal giving" response slightly more than those from Conservative homes, as the latter did slightly more than those from Reform homes. Discussion of Jewish topics in the parental home was inversely related to the "equal - equal" response.

The modal category of giving, where giving is considered an equally Jewish and American value but more is given to Jewish causes, was most positively associated with the level of observance in the parental home. Aside from this relationship, more Jewish attitudes on giving were generally inversely related to a higher level of Jewish background.

H. Camp

Both the proportion of Jews in the community where the respondent grew up and among the childhood friends of the respondent were highly related to choosing a Jewish camp environment (Table 7.11)[1]

Table 7.11: Camp: Mostly Jewish Campers and
Staff BY Background Jewish Density

	Community where Grew Up			Childhood Friends		
	half or more	some or none		all or most	half or fewer	
important	56.8	36.4		53.8	35.4	
unimportant	43.2	63.6		46.2	64.6	
column	125	99	224	145	79	224
totals	55.8	44.2	100%	64.7	35.3	100%
	gamma 0.39			gamma 0.36		

There was little difference among those from Orthodox, Conservative, or Reform homes, although a bit fewer of the latter chose the Jewish camp setting. The level of parental observance, the presence of Jewish objects and discussion of Jewish topics in the parental home were all positively associated with choosing the Jewish camp environment.

There was a positive linear relationship between the respondent's estimation of the importance of Jewish education and choosing the Jewish camp setting. Over sixty percent of those who considered their Jewish education a very important influence, 50.0% of those who considered it important, and 39.5% of those who felt it was not especially important found the Jewish composition of a prospective camp important.

Attitudes connected with continuity and group maintenance through the very personal medium of one's children thus return us to a situation of a clear positive association between attitudes and a broad range of Jewish background factors.

I. Observance

No major differences in observance emerged according to Jewish background factors. The relationship is most clearcut for parental observance and Jewish education. More respondents who come from homes in which the level of observance was high and who received more Jewish education are in the high observance category.

Those from Conservative homes observe the most and those from Orthodox homes the least. Those from Orthodox homes may feel the greatest need to reject the observance pattern of their parents (perhaps in part reflected by their having joined a Reform temple), while those from Conservative homes may have received a relatively traditional background that was sufficiently compatible with the American setting to avoid subsequent rejection.

II. Summary

A. Background Residential and Associational Concentration

The proportion of Jews in the community where the respondent grew up is positively related to the residential aspect of Particularism. The proportion of Jews among the respondent's childhood friends is most positively associated with the friendship measures of Particularism, and with the measure of identification with the Jewish group. Both the proportion of Jews in the community where the respondent grew up and among the respondent's childhood friends are positively associated with in-group feelings.

Israel is considered essential for the continuation of American Jewish life by more respondents who reported growing up in more Jewish communities and having mostly Jewish childhood friends. Respondents with these Jewish background characteristics are also somewhat more likely to oppose or discourage an intermarriage involving their children.[2]

Those who reported growing up in more Jewish communities, like those who currently live in more Jewish communities, are more likely to see anti-Semitism in the United States as a serious problem. More of the respondents who reported growing up in a community that was half or more Jewish and having all or mostly Jewish friends would choose a camp for their child where most of the campers and staff are Jewish.

Background Jewish density is thus positively associated with more Jewish attitudes across a broad range of dimensions centrally related to Jewish ethnicity.

However, those who reported growing up in relatively more Jewish communities, like those who currently live in more Jewish communities, observe Hanukkah, Passover, and the lighting of Sabbath candles somewhat *less* than do those who report growing up and currently living in less Jewish communities.

B. Jewishness of the Parental Home

A more Jewish home environment was positively related to in-group feelings and to higher expectations for the Jewishness of one's children. The Jewishness of the parental home was also positively associated with the Israel variables and with negative reaction to intermarriage. Those who reported growing up in more Jewish home environments saw anti-Semitism as a more serious problem and were more accepting of the idea that Jews are the chosen people.

A Jewish camp setting was preferred more by those who reported growing up in more Jewish home settings. Those whose parents observed more Jewish ritual and customs were themselves a bit more likely to observe Hanukkah, Passover, and the lighting of Sabbath candles.

The Jewishness of the parental home is thus also positively associated with more Jewish attitudes relating to several of the major dimensions of Jewish ethnicity.

142

Finally, those respondents whose parents defined themselves as Reform were as likely as those whose parents defined themselves as Orthodox or Conservative to accept the idea of chosenness and to express preference for giving to Jewish community causes. Fewer of those from Reform homes would react negatively to the prospective intermarriage of their child or felt it important that Israel be a spiritual homeland for world Jewry. More of those from Reform homes expressed the importance of Israel as a potential place of refuge for American Jews.

C. Jewish Education

A relatively higher level of Jewish education was positively associated with survivalist attitudes, with higher hopes for the Jewishness of one's children, with acceptance of the idea of chosenness, and with relatively more observance of Hanukkah, Passover, and Sabbath candles. It was inversely related to perceptions of the importance of Israel as both a spiritual homeland for world Jewry and a potential place of refuge for American Jews and to opposing or discouraging intermarriage.

The respondent's perception of the importance of Jewish education as an early influence affecting his/her current level of Jewishness was positively related to higher expectations for the Jewishness of one's children and to choosing a Jewish camp setting for one's child.

This association between estimates of the importance of one's own Jewish education and attitudes on factors affecting one's children is striking. Jewish education as a component of Jewish background is, however, positively associated with Jewish attitudes across a relatively narrow range of the central dimensions of Jewish ethnicity.

Overall, in viewing the relationship between Jewish background and attitudes, we note that *the expression of more Jewish attitudes is positively associated with a more Jewish background* particularly in terms of the proportion of Jews in the community in which the respondent grew up and among the respondent's childhood friends, and the Jewish content of the respondent's parental home (Table 7.12).

Table 7.12: Summary Statistical Table
Attitudes and Jewish Background*

	Jewsin Comm GrowUp gamma	Jews among Frnds GrowUp gamma	Self Def Parents gamma	Obs of Parents gamma	Jewish Objcts gamma	Discus Jewish Topics gamma	J. Ed gamma	J'ish Ed as Influence gamma
A. Particularism								
REACT J SUBURB	0.59							
% J WANT COMM.	0.67							
% FRIENDS BE J		0.26						
IMP. KIDS'FRNDS J	0.34	0.31						
B. Grp Belong&Id								
IDENTIFICATION		0.28						
SURVIVAL							0.30	
IN-GRP FEELING	0.19	0.25			0.28	0.41		
C. Hopes&Expec								
HOPES							0.20	0.18
EXPECTATIONS					0.25	0.38		0.18
D. Israel								
SPIRIT. HOMELAND			0.21					
REFUGE AM JEWS			-0.23				-0.24	
ESSEN AM J LIFE	0.17	0.28						
E. Intermarriage								
DO RE INTRMAR.				0.29		0.35		
TRANS. J'NESS						0.45		0.33
F. Anti-S&Chosen								
ANTI-S IN THE US			0.21			0.23		
JEWS CHOSEN			0.03	0.24	0.26		0.28	
G. Giving								
VALUE&RECIP								
H. Camp								
J CAMPERS&STAFF	0.39	0.36						0.29
I. Observance								
HANUK/PASSOVER /CANDLES	-0.13		0.04	0.15			0.18	

* selected crosstabulations

Notes

1. We should remember, however, that this was a minimalist response in terms of the Jewish nature of the camp. Sixty percent of the respondents considered the presence of Sabbath services unimportant, over 80% felt likewise about classes in Jewish religion or in Jewish history and culture, and over 90% in regard to the camp serving kosher food.

2. While those who grew up in *more* Jewish communities are more likely to express their concern about intermarriage as a threat to Judaism and the Jewish people, in terms of current Jewish density it is those who live in *less* Jewish communities that voice this same concern. Our attention is thus directed to the contrast between the Jewishness of the childhood community and that of the current community as a perception which potentially leads respondents to voice objection to intermarriage in terms of the threat posed to the Jewish future.

CHAPTER EIGHT

QUANTITATIVE ANALYSIS: STATISTICAL SUMMARY

I. Introduction

Bivariate analysis offers a clear picture of the existence of associations and an indication of the relative strength of relationships among background, density, and attitudes. This examination of specific associations is valuable in that it yields detail and particular insights which might be blurred or overlooked in more comprehensive summary measures.

Multivariate analysis, however, offers a distinct advantage over bivariate techniques. The strength of multivariate analysis lies in its ability to control for multiple intervening factors. With the use of multivariate analysis we can, for example, examine the association between background Jewish density and current Jewish density controlling for social characteristic variables.

Current Jewish density was highly associated in a positive relationship with background Jewish density and inversely with the level of secular education. Is the positive association between background Jewish density and current Jewish density maintained when controlled for the effects of secular education? Multivariate analysis allows us to answer this question.

Similarly, multivariate analysis permits us to examine the following critical associations:
–between current Jewish density and attitudes, controlling for background Jewish density and social characteristics;
–between background Jewish density and attitudes, controlling for current Jewish density and social characteristics; and
–between social characteristics and attitudes, controlling for both background and current Jewish density.

Are differences in Jewish background associated with differences in current Jewish density, or are the positive associations between these two measures accounted for by the effects of an intervening variable such as

145

secular education? Are differences in current patterns of residential and associational concentration associated with different attitudes in matters that relate centrally to Jewish ethnicity, or are the positive associations between Jewish density and attitudes spurious relationships, the result of differences in Jewish background or social characteristics?[1]

The measure of current Jewish density is that used throughout, a combined measure for the proportion of Jews in the respondent's community and among the respondent's friends. Jewish background enters the analysis as reported background Jewish density, the Jewish background component which bore the most consistent positive relationship with both current Jewish density and attitudes.

Secular education was chosen as the critical social characteristic measure because of the strength of its association with current Jewish density and with attitudes. The occupational prestige variable is not included in the multivariate analysis as it is highly correlated with secular education and therefore presents the problem of multicollinearity.[2] Variables of age and sex are, however, included: the former to test whether – within the age range included in the sample – patterns of association hold across age cohorts, and the latter as much prior research on Jewish ethnicity has virtually ignored the potential effects of gender differences.

The attitudinal measures analyzed are those discussed previously in light of their direct bearing on central aspects of Jewish ethnicity.

A summary scale comprised of several distinct variables was constructed for each attitudinal factor.[3] Multiple classification analysis was chosen as the preferred multivariate analysis technique, a procedure which indicates in straightforward fashion the strength of association between sets of variables, independent of (Eta) and controlled for (Beta) other factors.[4]

II. Findings

A. Jewish Density BY Background (Background Jewish Density, Education, Age, and Sex)

Current Jewish density was found to correlate highly with background

Jewish density[5] and with education (Table 8.1). Unadjusted for the other independent variables, the correlation between current Jewish density and background Jewish density is 0.34. Controlling for education, age, and sex reduces the strength of the correlation only minimally to 0.30. Further, the relationship between Jewish density and background Jewish density is monotonic; that is, each increment in background Jewish density is associated with an increment in current Jewish density.

Controlling for education, age, and sex, those in the high background Jewish density category are 0.23 below[6] the mean of current Jewish density, those in the mixed background Jewish density category 0.13 above the mean, and those in the low background Jewish density category 0.29 above the mean. In other words, the current Jewish density of those in the high background Jewish density category is greater than the average current Jewish density of the sample as a whole. The current Jewish density of those in the mixed background Jewish density category is less than the average of the sample as a whole and that of those in the low background Jewish density category even less. The difference between the high and the low categories of background Jewish density (-0.23 to 0.29, or 0.52) represents a variation of 28% around the mean of current Jewish density (1.84).

Thus the high positive association between background Jewish density and current Jewish density is maintained when controlled for the effects of education, age, and sex. Differences in background Jewish density are associated with differences in later residential and associational patterns.

The correlation between education and Jewish density is 0.30, which is reduced to 0.24 when controlled for background Jewish density, age, and sex. Except for the reversal within the highest categories of educational attainment ("some graduate study" and "graduate or professional degree") the relationship between Jewish density and education is also monotonic, and is an inverse relationship. That is, the higher the level of education, the lower the Jewish density. Controlled for background Jewish density, age, and sex, those with some college education or less are below the mean of Jewish density (indicating a greater degree of Jewish density), those who completed college are right at the mean, and those with at least some graduate study above the mean.

Table 8.1: Multiple Classification Analysis
Jewish Density BY Background
Jewish Density, Education, (Age, Sex)*

Grand mean = 1.84

Variable & Category	N	Unadjusted Dev'n	Eta	Adjusted for independents Dev'n	Beta
Background Jewish Density					
1 HI	107	-0.25		-0.23	
2 MIXED	57	0.11		0.13	
3 LO	57	0.36		0.29	
			0.34		0.30
Education					
1 H.S. OR LESS	9	-0.50		-0.37	
2 SOME COLLEGE	38	-0.39		-0.31	
3 COMPL.COLLEGE	52	0.01		0.00	
4 SOME GRAD STUDY	26	0.20		0.20	
5 GRAD OR PROF DEGREE	96	0.14		0.10	
			0.30		0.24

Multiple R^2 (includes Age and Sex)	0.18
Multiple R	0.42

* The details of Jewish density by age and sex are not
presented in the table as the correlation was not
significant. These factors are, however, taken into
account in the computation of the multiple R and
multiple R^2

Secular education is thus also highly associated with current Jewish density. The relation between secular education and Jewish density is, however, an inverse relationship: a higher level of secular education is associated with lower current Jewish density. This holds true when controlled for the effects of background Jewish density.

The correlations between Jewish density and age and between Jewish density and sex were insignificant. Together, however, the four independent variables account for eighteen percent of the variation in current Jewish density (Multiple $R^2 = 0.18$).

Differences in both background Jewish density and the level of educational attainment are strongly associated with differences in current patterns of Jewish residential and associational concentration. While the effects of Jewish background and secular education are in opposite directions, they appear to be largely independent effects as neither association is reduced to a major extent when controlled for the other.

We thus know that in this population of suburban Reform Jews we can expect to find those currently living in situations of higher Jewish density to report having grown up with higher proportions of Jews in their communities and among their friends and having a relatively lower level of secular education.

B. Attitudes BY Jewish Density and Background

Multiple classification analyses were carried out on all of the principal attitudinal dimensions by both current Jewish density and background factors.

1. The Particularism Scale (Table 8.2)

A very high correlation was revealed between particularism and Jewish density: 0.51 unadjusted and 0.44 adjusted for education, age, sex, and background Jewish density. A clear monotonic relationship emerges: controlling for the four background factors mentioned, those in the high Jewish density category are 1.39 below[7] the particularism mean, those in the mixed Jewish density category 0.63 above the mean, and those in the low Jewish density category 1.24 above. The difference between the high and low Jewish density categories (-1.39 to 1.24, or 2.63) represents a range of twenty-four percent around the mean of the Particularism Scale (10.91).

Those who currently live in situations of higher Jewish density thus hold more favorable attitudes towards Jewish particularism than do those who currently live in situations of lower Jewish density. This pattern of association holds even when controlled for background Jewish density and social characteristics. Whether this association is the result of the effects of Jewish density on attitudes, of a process of self-selection, or of a drive towards consistency, we do know that differences in current Jewish density are very highly associated with differences in attitudes towards Jewish particularism. Thus current Jewish density is positively associated with a central element of Jewish ethnicity pertaining to the distinction between group members and others.

Among the background factors, that with the highest correlation with particularism is the education variable. The correlation between education and particularism is 0.35 unadjusted and 0.23 net of the effects of current Jewish density, age, sex, and background Jewish density. Education is inversely related to particularism. The unadjusted deviations display a monotonic relationship between particularism and education, as do the adjusted deviations with the exception of a reversal between the "some college" and "completed college" categories. Controlling for Jewish density, age, sex, and background Jewish density, those with a college degree or less are below the particularism mean, those with some graduate education almost exactly at the mean, and those with a graduate or professional degree above the mean.

A higher level of secular education is thus associated with less particularistic attitudes even when controlled for other social characteristics, for background Jewish density, and for current Jewish density. The association of current Jewish density with particularism was reduced somewhat when controlled for education and other background variables. While the association between secular education and particularism is more significantly reduced when controlled for other background factors and for current Jewish density, secular education nonetheless emerges as an important factor in attitudes towards Jewish particularism.

Table 8.2: Multiple Classification Analysis
Particularism BY Jewish Density,
Education, (Age, sex), and
Background Jewish Density

Grand mean = 10.91

Variable & category	N	Unadjusted Dev'n	Eta	Adjusted for independents Dev'n	Beta
Jewish Density					
1 HI	83	-1.62		-1.39	
2 MIXED	91	0.72		0.63	
3 LO	47	1.47		1.24	
			0.51		0.44
Education					
1 H.S. OR LESS	9	-2.80		-2.01	
2 SOME COLLEGE	38	-0.88		-0.23	
3 COMPL.COLLEGE	52	-0.45		-0.42	
4 SOME GRAD STUDY	26	0.36		0.01	
5 GRAD OR PROF DEGREE	96	0.76		0.51	
			0.35		0.23
Background Jewish Density					
1 HI	107	-0.60		-0.16	
2 MIXED	57	-0.05		-0.17	
3 LO	57	1.18		0.47	
			0.29		0.11

Multiple R^2 (includes Age and Sex)　　0.33
Multiple R　　0.57

A positive correlation also emerges between background Jewish density and particularism: 0.29 unadjusted, but only 0.11 adjusted for current Jewish density, education, age, and sex. While differences in background Jewish density are thus associated with differences in attitudes towards Jewish particularism, the effects of background Jewish density appear to be mediated through other variables such as current Jewish density.

The unadjusted relationship between background Jewish density and particularism is monotonic; adjusted for the other independent variables, there is virtually no difference between the high and mixed background Jewish density categories, though a clear difference remains between these and the low background Jewish density category. The former are 0.16 and 0.17 below the mean respectively while the latter is 0.47 above.

No significant correlation emerged between the Particularism Scale and age or sex.

The combined effects of current Jewish density, education, age, sex, and background Jewish density account for thirty-three percent of the variation in particularism, primarily as a function of the effects of current Jewish density, education, and background Jewish density.

A major portion of the explainable variation on this central dimension of Jewish ethnicity is thus accounted for by variables of current Jewish density, education, and background Jewish density. While the effects of current Jewish density and secular education appear to be direct, that of background Jewish density seems to be mediated through other factors, most probably through current Jewish density.

2. The Belonging and Identification Scale (Table 8.3)

A fairly strong correlation emerged between the Belonging and Identification Scale and Jewish density. The unadjusted correlation of 0.22 decreases only minimally to 0.19 when controlled for education, age, sex, and background Jewish density.

The similarity in the relationship of Jewish density to particularism and of Jewish density to group belonging, despite the weaker nature of the latter association, shows that a consistent pattern holds in the association of Jewish density with these two key attitudinal scales. As was the case with the Particularism Scale, the relation between Jewish density and the Belonging and Identification Scale is also monotonic: controlling for the remaining independent variables, those in the high Jewish density category are 0.32 below[8] the mean, those in the mixed category of Jewish density 0.05 below the mean, and those in the low Jewish density category 0.66 above. The difference between the high and low categories of Jewish density (-0.32 to 0.66, or 0.98) represents a deviation of eighteen percent around the mean Belonging and Identification score (5.37).

The correlations of education, age, sex, and background Jewish density with the Belonging and Identification Scale were much less strong. Both education and background Jewish density bore a correlation of 0.09 with this attitudinal scale. Noteworthy in regard to these two relationships is the following:
– the correlations of education and background Jewish density with this attitudinal measure are once again, as was the case with the particularism measure, weaker than that of Jewish density but stronger than those of age and sex;
– in terms of education, the only group significantly above the mean is that with a "graduate or professional degree." (The group furthest below the mean is that with only a high school education or less.[9])
– in terms of background Jewish density, while the correlation is weak, the relationship is monotonic. Those in the high and mixed background Jewish density categories are below the mean and those in the low background Jewish density category above.

While correlations were weaker and the percentage of variation accounted for lower than in the case of the Particularism Scale, the same pattern which emerged in regard to particularism also holds for the Belonging and Identification Scale. Current Jewish density is the factor most highly associated with group belonging and identification, followed by secular education and background Jewish density. The correlation of Jewish density with the attitudinal measure is reduced only slightly when controlled for Jewish background and social characteristics, while the correlations of secular education and background Jewish density with the attitudinal measure are reduced more substantially when controlled for the effects of current Jewish density and other background variables.

Table 8.3: Multiple Classification Analysis
Group Belonging and Identification
BY Jewish Density, Education,
(Age, Sex), and Background Jewish
Density

Grand mean = 5.37

variable & category	N	unadjusted Dev'n	Eta	Adjusted for independents Dev'n	Beta
Jewish Density					
1 HI	83	-0.44		-0.32	
2 MIXED	91	0.02		-0.05	
3 LO	47	0.74		0.66	
			0.22		0.19
Education					
1 H.S. OR LESS	9	-0.82		-0.46	
2 SOME COLLEGE	38	-0.34		-0.06	
3 COMPL.COLLEGE	52	0.01		0.03	
4 SOME GRAD STUDY	26	-0.26		-0.32	
5 GRAD OR PROF DEGREE	96	0.27		0.14	
			0.15		0.09
Background Jewish Density					
1 HI	107	-0.26		-0.11	
2 MIXED	57	-0.04		-0.07	
3 LO	57	0.52		0.29	
			0.16		0.09

Multiple R^2 (includes Age and Sex)   0.08
Multiple R   0.27

The similarity in the pattern of association comes not as a surprise, but rather as confirmation of the previous description of particularism and identification as relating to two central elements of Jewish ethnicity – consciousness of kind and the distinction between group members and others – seen to represent two sides of the same coin.

3. The Intermarriage Scale (Table 8.4)

Jewish density was also found to correlate highly with reactions to the prospect of an intermarriage involving one's child: the unadjusted correlation of 0.27 remained stable at 0.28 when controlled for education, age, sex, and background Jewish density. Once again, the relationship was monotonic, with those in the high Jewish density category 0.29 below the mean (indicating a stronger negative reaction to intermarriage), those in the mixed Jewish density category 0.02 below the mean, and those in the low Jewish density category 0.56 above, when controlled for the remaining independent variables. The difference between the high and low categories (-0.29 to 0.56, or 0.85) represents a deviation of twenty-two percent around the mean Intermarriage Scale score (3.95).

The attitude towards intermarriage, perceived as a critical element in group maintenance, is thus positively associated with current Jewish density. Those living in situations of higher Jewish density express more negative reactions to intermarriage regardless of their background Jewish density or social characteristic profile.

Education was once again coupled with Jewish density as an important independent variable. The correlation of education with intermarriage was 0.17 unadjusted and 0.15 adjusted for the other independent variables. Once again the effects of Jewish density and secular education appear as independent effects.

Background Jewish density, however, was not found to correlate highly with the Intermarriage Scale. Nor was sex strongly associated with the reaction to intermarriage. Rather, the independent variable found to correlate with the Intermarriage Scale to a degree second only to Jewish density was age: 0.23 unadjusted and 0.21 adjusted for Jewish density, education, sex, and background Jewish density. While the oldest and youngest of the three age cohorts were above the mean, the middle age

156

Table 8.4: Multiple Classification Analysis
Intermarriage BY Jewish Density,
Education, Age, (Sex, and
Background Jewish Density)

Grand mean = 3.95

Variable & category	N	Unadjusted Dev'n	Eta	Adjusted for independents Dev'n	Beta
Jewish Density					
1 HI	83	-0.29		-0.29	
2 MIXED	91	-0.03		-0.02	
3 LO	47	0.56		0.56	
			0.27		0.28
Education					
1 H.S. OR LESS	9	-0.84		-0.61	
2 SOME COLLEGE	38	0.10		0.20	
3 COMPL COLLEGE	52	-0.05		-0.03	
4 SOME GRAD STUDY	26	-0.14		-0.20	
5 GRAD OR PROF DEGREE	96	0.10		0.05	
			0.17		0.15
Age					
1 OLDEST (50-59)	45	0.16		0.19	
2 MIDDLE (40-49)	121	-0.23		-0.22	
3 YOUNGEST (30-39)	55	0.38		0.32	
			0.23		0.21

Multiple R^2 (includes Sex and Background Jewish Den.)   0.15
Multiple R   0.38

cohort was 0.22 below. We remember that it was this group aged 40-49, which has the most children of dating age, that reacted most negatively to the prospect of intermarriage.

The combined effects of Jewish density, education, age, sex, and background Jewish density account for fifteen percent of the variation in the response to intermarriage.

Differences in current Jewish density are once again associated with differences along a critical attitudinal dimension. In terms of social characteristics, while secular education proved once again to be important, differences in attitudes towards intermarriage seem to be more directly related to age-specific concerns.

4. Camp (Table 8.5)

Jewish density and education were also found to correlate highly with the other attitudinal measure which, in addition to intermarriage, deals explicitly with children, namely, the importance attributed to a Jewish camp environment.

The unadjusted correlation of Jewish density and preference for a Jewish camp setting is 0.31; adjusted 0.26. Further, the relationship is once again monotonic: those in the high Jewish density category are 0.29 below the mean (indicating a higher position on the camp measure), those in the mixed category 0.02 above the mean, and those in the low Jewish density category 0.35 above. The difference between the high and low categories of Jewish density (-0.19 to 0.35, or 0.54) represents a deviation of twenty-three percent around the mean camp score (2.37).

While background Jewish density correlated with the camp attitude to some extent in a relationship that was also monotonic, the strongest correlation was found between camp and education. Those in the highest education category expressed the least Jewish preference in regard to camp; the overall relationship between camp and education was not, however, monotonic. Nonetheless, the 0.39 correlation of education and camp controlled for Jewish density, age, sex, and background Jewish density is striking.

158

Table 8.5: Multiple Classification Analysis
Camp BY Jewish Density, Education,
(Age, Sex), and Background Jewish
Density

Grand mean = 2.37

Variable & category	N	Unadjusted Dev'n	Eta	Adjusted for independents Dev'n	Beta
Jewish Density					
1 HI	50	-0.25		-0.19	
2 MIXED	66	0.07		0.02	
3 LO	23	0.37		0.35	
			0.31		0.26
Education					
1 H.S.OR LESS	7	-0.23		-0.14	
2 SOME COLLEGE	24	-0.04		0.11	
3 COMPL COLLEGE	29	-0.37		-0.34	
4 SOME GRAD STUDY	14	-0.37		-0.50	
5 GRAD OR PROF DEGREE	65	0.29		0.23	
			0.41		0.39
Background Jewish Density					
1 HI	64	-0.14		-0.06	
2 MIXED	36	-0.04		-0.03	
3 LO	39	0.27		0.13	
			0.24		0.12

Multiple R^2 (includes Age and Sex)   0.26
Multiple R   0.51

Overall, twenty-six percent of the variation in the camp preference measure is accounted for by the combined effects of the five independent variables.

5. The Israel Scale (Table 8.6)

Another set of attitudes found to correlate highly with Jewish density and education were those towards Israel's potential roles and the essentiality of Israel for American Jewish life.

The correlation of Jewish density and attitudes towards Israel adjusted for the effects of education, age, sex, and background Jewish density was 0.14 (down from 0.19 unadjusted). Those in the high Jewish density category were below the mean (indicating a higher position on the Israel Scale) and those in the mixed and low Jewish density categories above. The relationship was not, however, monotonic as those in the mixed density category were in a lower position on the scale than were those in the low density group.

The independent variable found to correlate most strongly with the Israel Scale was education. The unadjusted correlation of 0.27 fell only minimally to 0.25 when adjusted for Jewish density, age, sex, and background Jewish density. The relationship was not, however, monotonic.

Neither age, sex, nor background Jewish density correlated highly with the Israel Scale. Overall, the combined effects of the five independent variables account for twelve percent of the variation in the Israel Scale. Though a relatively low percentage of variation in the Israel Scale is accounted for, the strongest associations are again between the attitudinal measure and Jewish density and education.

6. Anti-Semitism (Table 8.7)

Twenty-four percent of the variation in the attitude towards the

Table 8.6: Multiple Classification Analysis
Israel BY Jewish Density,
Education, (Age, Sex, and
Background Jewish Density)

Grand mean = 7.72

Variable & category	N	Unadjusted Dev'n	Eta	Adjusted for independents Dev'n	Beta
Jewish Density					
1 HI	83	-0.54		-0.42	
2 MIXED	91	0.49		0.35	
3 LO	47	0.00		0.06	
			0.19		0.14
Education					
1 H.S. OR LESS	9	1.17		1.34	
2 SOME COLLEGE	38	-0.27		0.06	
3 COMPL COLLEGE	52	-0.95		-0.90	
4 SOME GRAD STUDY	26	-0.26		-0.32	
5 GRAD OR PROF DEGREE	96	0.58		0.43	
			0.27		0.25

Multiple R^2 (includes Age, Sex, and Bgrnd Jewish Den.)   0.12
Multiple R   0.34

Table 8.7: Multiple Classification Analysis
Anti-Semitism BY Jewish Density,
Education, (Age, Sex, and
Background Jewish Density)

Grand mean = 2.43

Variable & category	N	Unadjusted Dev'n	Eta	Adjusted for independents Dev'n	Beta
Jewish Density					
1 HI	50	-0.29		-0.22	
2 MIXED	66	0.17		0.13	
3 LO	23	0.13		0.11	
			0.35		0.26
Education					
1 H.S. OR LESS	7	-0.15		-0.08	
2 SOME COLLEGE	24	-0.35		-0.20	
3 COMPL COLLEGE	29	-0.26		-0.23	
4 SOME GRAD STUDY	14	0.14		0.10	
5 GRAD OR PROF DEGREE	65	0.23		0.16	
			0.40		0.28

Multiple R^2 (includes Age, Sex, and Bgrnd Jewish Den.)   0.24
Multiple R   0.49

seriousness of anti-Semitism in the United States was explained by the combined effects of the five independent variables tested.

The strongest correlations were once again with Jewish density and education (0.26 and 0.28 respectively controlled for the remaining four independent variables in each case). Neither relationship was monotonic. A pattern did emerge, however, as those in the high Jewish density category were below[1] the mean and those in the mixed and low Jewish density categories above, while those in the lower three education categories were below the mean and those in the higher two categories above.

Jewish density is thus positively, and secular education inversely associated with another attitudinal dimension relating to the distinction between members of the Jewish group and outsiders.

7. Giving (Table 8.8)

Although a rather small percentage of the variation in attitudes towards giving[2] was explained by the five independent variables, the correlations do fit into the general pattern which has developed.

Attitudes towards giving were found to correlate most highly with Jewish density, education, and background Jewish density. The adjusted correlation with Jewish density was 0.17 and the relationship was monotonic with those in the high Jewish density category ranking highest and those in the low Jewish density category lowest. The relationship between giving and education was not monotonic; the adjusted correlation was 0.14.

The independent variable which correlated most highly with giving was background Jewish density. The unadjusted correlation of 0.18 rose to 0.21 when controlled for the effects of Jewish density, education, age, and sex. The relationship was monotonic, but inverse with those in the low background Jewish density category *below* the mean (indicating a more particularistic Jewish attitude towards giving) and those in the mixed and high background Jewish density categories above.

The picture which emerges in relation to attitudes towards giving is thus mixed. Like many of the other attitudinal measures, attitudes towards

Table 8.8: Multiple Classification Analysis Giving BY Jewish Density, Education, (Age, Sex), and Background Jewish Density

Grand mean= 1.96

Variable & category	N	Unadjusted Dev'n	Eta	Adjusted for independents Dev'n	Beta
Jewish Density					
1 HI	50	0.00		-0.11	
2 MIXED	66	-0.05		-0.02	
3 LO	23	0.13		0.29	
			0.08		0.17
Education					
1 H.S. OR LESS	7	0.04		-0.02	
2 SOME COLLEGE	24	0.17		0.22	
3 COMPL COLLEGE	29	-0.03		-0.05	
4 SOME GRAD STUDY	14	-0.17		-0.19	
5 GRAD OR PROF DEGREE	65	-0.02		-0.02	
			0.12		0.14
Background Jewish Density					
1 HI	64	0.11		0.13	
2 MIXED	36	0.04		0.05	
3 LO	39	-0.21		-0.26	
			0.18		0.21

Multiple R^2 (includes Age and Sex) 0.07
Multiple R 0.26

giving are most strongly associated with current Jewish density, secular education, and background Jewish density.

However, while there is a positive relationship between current Jewish density and more Jewish attitudes towards giving, there is an inverse relationship between attitudes towards giving and background Jewish density. The role which giving has assumed in the American Jewish community and its potential impact on these associations has been discussed previously. These associations and their relation to other findings will be dealt with below in the summary of this chapter.

8. Observance (Table 8.9)

The combined measure for observance of Hanukkah, Passover, and the lighting of Sabbath candles correlated most strongly with current Jewish density and education. The adjusted correlation was in each case 0.24, though neither relationship was monotonic. The correlation of observance and sex was 0.11 adjusted for the effects of the other independent variables, with females having a higher position than males on this scale of observance.

9. Chosenness, Hopes and Expectations

The percentage of variation accounted for by the five independent variables was lower in the cases of chosenness and hopes and expectations than for any of the other variables tested.

Chosenness correlated highly with age (0.18 adjusted). The relationship was monotonic, with the youngest age cohort most agreeing that Jews are the chosen people. Hopes and expectations for the Jewishness of one's children correlated most highly with Jewish density (0.16 adjusted) and sex (0.14 adjusted). The former relationship was not monotonic, and females had higher hopes and expectations than males.

III. Summary

Both background Jewish density and secular education were found to be strongly associated with current Jewish density. The relationship between background Jewish density and current Jewish density is positive, while that between secular education and current Jewish density

Table 8.9: Multiple Classification Analysis
Observance BY Jewish Density, Education,
(Age), Sex, and (Background Jewish Density)

Grand mean = 1.63

Variable & category	N	Unadjusted Dev'n	Eta	Adjusted for independents Dev'n	Beta
Jewish Density					
1 HI	50	0.07		0.01	
2 MIXED	66	-0.13		-0.12	
3 LO	23	0.24		0.31	
			0.22		0.24
Education					
1 H.S. OR LESS	7	-0.35		-0.37	
2 SOME COLLEGE	24	0.24		0.29	
3 COMPL COLLEGE	29	-0.01		-0.02	
4 SOME GRAD STUDY	14	0.01		0.00	
5 GRAD OR PROF DEGREE	65	-0.05		-0.06	
			0.21		0.24
Sex					
1 MALE	70	0.02		0.07	
2 FEMALE	69	-0.02		-0.07	
			0.04		0.11

Multiple R² (includes Age and Background Jewish Den.)   0.11
Multiple R   0.33

is inverse. The effects of background Jewish density and secular education on current Jewish density appear to be largely independent of each other.

The findings which emerge from the multivariate analyses of attitudes by background Jewish density, social characteristics, and current Jewish density are summarized in Table 8.10. Certain patterns are clearly visible.

A high percentage of the variation was accounted for in the cases of the particularism, camp, and anti-Semitism measures. In each instance, the attitudinal dependent variable correlated most highly with Jewish density and education. The relationship with education was not monotonic in any of these three cases. The relationship between Jewish density and particularism and camp was monotonic; in the relationship between Jewish density and anti-Semitism, it was also the high Jewish density category that had the highest position on the anti-Semitism variable.

Thus current Jewish density is clearly and strongly associated in a positive relationship with attitudinal measures which address the issues of the distinction between Jews and others and of group continuity through the next generation. While the pattern of association of secular education with these attitudinal measures is less clearcut, the general direction is that higher levels of secular education are associated with less positive Jewish attitudes on these dimensions of Jewish ethnicity.

Jewish density also correlated highly in a monotonic relationship with intermarriage, belonging and identification, and giving. In each case on these measures pertaining to group maintenance and consciousness of kind, higher current Jewish density is associated with more positive Jewish attitudes.

Additionally, Jewish density correlated highly with observance, hopes and expectations, and attitudes towards Israel. Though the relation was non-monotonic, the general pattern which emerges for these variables which relate to the common cultural heritage of the group and to group continuity is that higher current Jewish density is once again associated with more positive Jewish attitudes.

Table 8.10: Summary Statistical Table
Multiple Classification Analysis:
Attitudes By Background Jewish
Density, Social Characteristics,
Current Jewish Density*

Depend Vars	Jewish Den c^1	m^2	Education c	m	Background Jewish Den c	m	Age c	m	Sex c	% var acctd for R^2
PARTIC	0.44	yes	0.23	no	0.11	no	0.05	yes	0.09	0.33
BLONG	0.19	yes	0.09	no	0.09	yes	0.02	**	0.07	0.08
INTMAR	0.28	yes	0.15	no	0.02	**	0.21	no	0.02	0.15
CAMP	0.26	yes	0.39	no	0.12	yes	0.10	yes	0.08	0.26
ISRAEL	0.14	no	0.25	no	0.07	yes	0.08	no	0.05	0.12
ANTI-S	0.26	no	0.28	no	0.14	no	0.11	no	0.08	0.24
GIVING	0.17	yes	0.14	no	0.21	yes	0.03	**	0.06	0.07
OBSERV	0.24	no	0.24	no	0.05	**	0.07	**	0.11	0.11
CHOSEN	0.09	**	0.05	**	0.08	**	0.18	yes	0.10	0.04
HOPE/EX	0.16	no	0.11	no	0.10	no	0.05	no	0.14	0.06

*All figures are adjusted scores.
**Too little variation to be meaningful.
[1] correlation
[2] monotonic

Education also correlated highly with attitudes towards Israel, observance, intermarriage, and giving. Those in the higher educational categories rank lower on these attitudinal measures. Patterns of association
between secular education and attitudes were, however, much less consistent than those between Jewish density and attitudes.

Background Jewish density correlated most highly with attitudes towards anti-Semitism and giving. It was, however, those who report
having grown up in situations of high background Jewish density that
consider anti-Semitism a less serious problem and that express the least
particularistic attitudes towards giving. This combination is perhaps
indicative of what might be termed a negative mode of Jewish identification on the part of those who report having grown up in situations
of lower Jewish density. Their impetus to identification may originate
largely in perceptions of hostility directed at the Jewish group. They
may also perceive of participation in Jewish life as subsumed to a disproportionate degree under the mechanism of giving, as a way of feeling
that one has fulfilled the obligation without actually devoting much time
or effort to more involving aspects of participation in the life and culture
of the group.

Background Jewish density also had a monotonic relationship with attitudes towards belonging and identification, camp, and Israel. Those
who reported coming from a background of higher Jewish density express more positive attitudes along these dimensions that address consciousness of being members of the group, group continuity, and shared
cultural heritage.

Age correlated highly with the intermarriage and chosenness measures.
The correlation of age with the former reflects the concerns of parents
with children of dating age. The greater acceptance of chosenness by
the younger respondents may reflect the recent increase in the perceived
legitimacy of ethnic identification. Further evidence on this point would,
however, be necessary before such a case could be convincingly made.

Sex correlated most highly with the measure of hopes and expectations
for the Jewishness of one's children and with the measure of observance.
In these, as in most of the attitudinal variables tested, despite low cor-

relations, females expressed more Jewish positions than males.

Thus, current Jewish density bears the strongest, most consistent positive linear relationship with the attitudinal measures tested. While education also correlated highly with the majority of attitudes examined, no decisive pattern of relationship emerged. The unadjusted correlations of background Jewish density and attitudinal measures were significantly reduced when controlled for current Jewish density and social characteristics.

Returning to the central research questions posed at the beginning of this study, we can therefore note that the Jewishness of the respondent's early environment in the form of reported background residential and associational concentration is positively associated with higher current Jewish density even when controlled for selected social characteristics of the respondents, most especially for secular education.

Further, differences in current residential and associational patterns are associated with different attitudes in matters that relate centrally to Jewish ethnicity: higher current Jewish density is associated with more positive Jewish attitudes, especially along the dimensions of identification with the Jewish group, distinction between Jews and others, and group maintenance and continuity. Background Jewish density seems to have less of a direct effect on attitudes. Rather, the effect of background Jewish density on attitudes appears to be mediated through other variables, most particularly through the effect of background Jewish density on current Jewish density.

170

Notes

1. The possibility also exists that these relationships are influenced by intervening variables other than those taken into account. Nonetheless, analyzing these relationships in terms of the net strength of each association adjusted for intervening factors which have proven significant in the findings previously presented allows us much more confidently to address the key issues which underlie this research.

2. Multicollinearity is a problem encountered when two or more independent variables are highly intercorrelated. It leads to overlap in the explained variance on the dependent variable and therefore to lack of clarity in interpretation. One of the suggested solutions to the problem of multicollinearity is to use only one of the variables in the highly correlated set to represent the common underlying dimension (Norman H. Nie et al., *Statistical Package for the Social Sciences* (SPSS), New York: McGraw-Hill, 1975, p. 341.)

3. Thus the "Particularism Scale" was constructed by assigning one point to the "most Jewish" of the three possible responses on each of the principal variables associated with the Particularism factor, two points to the second "most Jewish" response, and three points to the "least Jewish" response. A similar process was used to create a "Belonging and Identification" scale, a "Hopes and Expectations" scale, an "Israel" scale, and an "Intermarriage" scale.

4. See Nie et al., *SPSS*, pp. 409-410, 416-418. In addition to unadjusted and adjusted correlations, multiple classification analysis also yields deviations from the mean of the dependent variable for each category of each independent variable. This reveals the position of each category of the independent variable on each dependent variable, both without and with adjustment for intervening factors. Finally, this technique tells us how much of the total variation in each dependent variable is accounted for by the combined effects of the independent variables (Multiple R^2).

5. Background Jewish density is a combined measure for the proportion of Jews in the community in which the respondent grew up and among the respondent's childhood friends.

6. A *lower* figure indicates *higher* Jewish density as the values of the Jewish density variable were coded "1. HI 2. MIXED 3.LO".

7. Again, a lower figure represents a higher rank on the Particu-

larism Scale.

8. Once again, a lower figure indicates a higher position on the scale.

9. The apparent significance of the contrast between this group and its opposite extreme is, however, mitigated by the fact that the small N makes this relationship statistically unstable and that the other group significantly below the mean is that with "some graduate study."

10. A lower figure once again indicates a higher position on the scale.

11. As in the preceding chapters, the "giving" variable is a combined measure dealing with the source of the value and the recipient.

CHAPTER NINE

QUALITATIVE ANALYSIS: PROFILES OF AMERICAN REFORM JEWS

Profiles I

To flesh out the statistical skeleton and convey more fully a sense of the complex nuances of being a Jew in American society, it will be useful to sketch a series of profiles emerging from the data analysis.

The impetus for the construction of profiles originated in a sense that a number of related but distinct types existed among the pool of respondents. This impression originated in prior contact with the communities and the two temple memberships sampled. It was strengthened during the course of coding the returned questionnaires with the emergence of consistent patterns of response. These impressions of the ethnographer's and coder's eye were later confirmed by evidence from the data.

The profiles *do not represent actual individual respondents.* Rather, the profiles constitute *composite ideal types* serving to summarize and concretize the general thrust of findings.

While legitimate reservations exist about the process of translating quantitative data into artificial constructs, these profiles are not misleading averages of extreme variations. Rather, they depict representative patterns among the respondents and render the quantitative findings more intelligible and manageable through adding another dimension to the quantitative skeleton.

We begin our profiles with *Mr. Abrams, a Jewish particularist.* He is thirty-eight years old, married with two children ages ten and six. Both he and his wife are the grandchildren of east European immigrants. The Abrams family lives in a community which Mr. Abrams describes as mostly Jewish. Mr. and Mrs. Abrams have both completed college, but neither holds an advanced degree. Mrs. Abrams is not currently employed; Mr. Abrams works as the sales manager of a local manufacturing firm, where his annual salary is just over $40,000.

Mr. Abrams grew up in a mostly Jewish community where almost all of his childhood friends were Jewish. He remembers his parents having observed a rather high level of Jewish ritual and customs while he was growing up; his wife recalls a similar level of observance in her parental home. In addition, Mr. Abrams remembers both the presence of Jewish artifacts and the discussion of Jewish topics in his parents' home. Both Mr. Abrams and his wife received a relatively high level of Jewish education, attending afternoon Hebrew schools for several years.

Mr. Abrams feels that his parental home was a very important early influence on his current level of Jewishness and that his childhood friends and Jewish education were also important such influences.

Mrs. Bloom, a Jewish survivalist, is fifty, and describes her community as comprised of only some Jewish families. Both she and her husband, who currently have only one of their children living at home with them, are themselves the children of east European parents who arrived in the United States at a young age.

Mrs. Bloom's husband is a professor in the natural sciences at a local university; Mrs. Bloom, who holds a master's degree in social work, is currently employed in a social service agency. Their combined annual income is just over $60,000.

Mrs. Bloom grew up in a community where less than half of the population was Jewish. Her parents, though first generation, grew up in the United States and by the time Mrs. Bloom was growing up identified as Reform Jews.

Neither Mrs. Bloom nor her husband think of their parents' level of observance as having been high while they were growing up. Mrs. Bloom remembers neither the presence of Jewish objects nor the discussion of Jewish topics in her parents' home. In Mrs. Bloom's eyes, neither her parental home nor her early Jewish education were important influences on her current level of Jewishness.

Most, but not all, of the friends of both Mr. Abrams and Mrs. Bloom are Jewish.[1]

Mr. Abrams holds what may be called very Jewish attitudes. Not only does he actually live in a mostly Jewish community and have mostly Jewish friends, he clearly feels this is as it should be. Both the Jewish composition of his community and the presence of the temple played positive roles in his choosing to live where he does. He definitely feels that Jews should be in the majority in his community and would in fact not react negatively to his community becoming an all Jewish suburb. Asked why the proportion of Jews would make a difference in choosing a new community should he move, Mr. Abrams responds:

> I like living with my people, am more comfortable with my own people, most comfortable in a Jewish atmosphere. We have more in common and similar values, common interests, backgrounds, beliefs.
> I want to be with my own – I want *my children* to be with their own. I want my children growing up being exposed to other Jewish families. A high Jewish concentration is more conducive to children remaining Jewish.
> A high proportion of Jews can support Jewish institutions in the community and establish a Jewish community feeling. In this atmosphere I feel my ethnic roots.[2]

Mr. Abrams feels that an American Jew should have mostly Jewish friends and not at all surprisingly it is very important to him that most of his children's friends also be Jewish. He would not, however, feel that someone was not a "good Jew" if most of that person's friends were not Jewish.

Although he does not always observe the most widely observed Jewish holidays, transmitting his Jewish heritage to his children is a very important factor in Mr. Abrams's celebration of Jewish holidays and observance of Jewish customs. Mr. Abrams feels that his children will probably be less Jewish than he hopes they might be. Nonetheless, in his effort to provide them with a Jewish environment, in choosing a camp for his children Mr. Abrams would look for one in which most of the other campers and staff were Jewish. Jewish day schools, however, are another matter, and while he would not send his own children to one, Mr. Abrams believes that:

> Everyone should have a choice. If people want to send their
> children to Jewish day schools they should be able to. It's
> good for those who want it. I don't like the idea for my
> own children – but think it's okay for those who want it.
> The real world is diverse and we have to learn to live in it.
> Secular education is vital, supplemented by religious school.
> The same can be accomplished with a strong family, religious
> school, and a religious camp.

Mr. Abrams does not accept the idea that the Jews are the chosen people.
He would, however, feel negatively should one of his children consider
marrying a non-Jew and would try to discourage such an intermarriage,
phrasing his opposition in terms of the marital problems which are likely
to arise. He would explain to his child that:

> Marriage is difficult enough without problems like religion,
> without an added burden. The institution of marriage is
> a difficult prospect for most young couples; a religion factor
> only complicates communication because of the differences in
> tradition that affect their family and relations with in-laws.

Mr. Abrams feels himself highly identified with the Jews as a group. He
feels both closer to and a sense of greater responsibility for other Jews
than for other non-Jewish Americans. He is offended in a strong personal
sense whenever he hears negative comment about Jews. Such comments
do not come as any great surprise to Mr. Abrams as he considers anti-
Semitism a fairly serious problem in the United States.

Israel is an important aspect of Mr. Abrams's identity as an American
Jew. He is convinced that Israel's continued existence is essential for
Jewish life in America and considers Israel very important as a spiritual
and cultural center for world Jewry, as an actual place of refuge for Jews
in distress, and as a potential place of refuge for American Jews.

Mr. Abrams favors giving more to Jewish causes although he acknowl-
edges that charity, though different from *tzedakkah*, is a basic American
value.

Mrs. Bloom's attitudes are far more mixed than those of Mr. Abrams.
Although she lives in a community in which Jews are the minority, she

does have mostly Jewish friends. This mixture of low residential and high friendship concentration is reflected in her attitudes on the subject of Jewish community.

In regard to the choice of her present community, Mrs. Bloom wanted to live in an area in which a Jewish community exists and where there is a temple. However, she also wanted a community that was mixed in terms of the ethnic and religious backgrounds of its residents. In choosing a new community in which to live should she move, Mrs. Bloom would once again opt for a mixed community, but for reasons that include positive Jewish sentiments. She explains:

> It's most important to have a community of Jews but also to be able to get along in the gentile world and be proud of Jewish identity in the face of all the others, to be able to participate in Jewish culture without becoming part of a "ghetto." I definitely would want a viable Jewish community yet in some proportion to the real world. There is more appreciation of one another in this proportion. I want to feel comfortable yet live realistically.
> While I feel comfortable in a Jewish neighborhood, my ties with friends have been established to a degree that I don't need to be "surrounded" by only Jews. I would still maintain membership in the Temple although my children no longer need religious education. "Some" Jews is more like the reality of the world – too few would lead to a feeling of isolation. It should be a comfortable ethnic mix; I would not want to lose the familiarity of Jewish customs and ideas.

Mrs. Bloom would react negatively should the community in which she presently lives reach the "tipping-point" and face the prospect of becoming an all Jewish suburb. In spite of her actually having mostly Jewish friends herself, she claims that the proportion of Jews among friends of an American Jew does not matter and makes no difference as to whether or not one is considered a "good Jew." She is, however, a bit less unequivocal in regard to the friendship pattern of her one child who still lives at home and simply cannot take a decisive stand on the issue of whether or not it is important that most of his friends be Jewish.

Mrs. Bloom's relatively more Jewish attitudes in matters that concern children are also reflected in other ways. She always observes Hanukkah and Passover, holidays that are clearly child-centered in the observance patterns of American Jews, and also usually lights Sabbath candles. Transmitting Jewishness to her children continues to serve as a very important motivation behind Mrs. Bloom's Jewish celebration and observance.

Like Mr. Abrams, Mrs. Bloom hopes that her children will be more Jewish than she actually expects they will be. Unlike Mr. Abrams, whether or not a camp had mostly Jewish campers and staff was not an important consideration in Mrs. Bloom's choosing the camps to which she sent her children. Mrs. Bloom does not feel strongly one way or the other about Jewish day schools, though more of her friends in situations similar to her own oppose than favor them.

Mrs. Bloom rejects the concept of Jewish chosenness, though like Mr. Abrams she would both react negatively if her unmarried son proposed to marry a non-Jew and would try to discourage him from doing so. She would state her opposition, however, in terms of the potential threat which intermarriage poses to the Jewish people and to Judaism on both a personal and collective level.

> The continuation of the Jewish people is important to me. Judaism will never continue in future generations with intermarriage because intermarriage is the most serious threat to the existence of the Jewish people. I wouldn't want my child to depart from Jewish values and lifestyle. I also feel a responsibility to the Jewish people for future generations. Being Jewish is special. Having a grandchild "mixed" would be a great loss in maintaining the Jewish feeling. I want any children brought up Jewish, would not want to see them attend church. Judaism is a way of life and culture that must be preserved. I would not want to accomplish through intermarriage what Hitler failed to do in the Holocaust.

Mrs. Bloom does identify with the Jewish people, as is obvious from her statements above, but somewhat less strongly so than Mr. Abrams. She clearly considers herself a Jewish survivalist although she is not always willing to support those positions and engage in those behaviors which are apparently most conducive to Jewish survival. She sees anti-Semitism as a problem of moderate proportions in the United States.

Personally, Mrs. Bloom feels that the existence of Israel is essential for Jewish life in America, though once again her attitude in this regard is a bit stronger than that of most of her similarly situated friends. Mrs. Bloom sees Israel primarily as a spiritual homeland and a place of refuge for Jews outside of the United States who may be in distress, and less as a center of Jewish culture or a potential place of refuge for American Jews. The latter is in keeping with her relatively lower estimation of the seriousness of anti-Semitism in the United States.

Finally, despite her somewhat more mixed attitudes, Mrs. Bloom definitely prefers giving to Jewish causes and is hard put to decide whether giving is more a Jewish value or equally Jewish and American.

Profiles II[3]

Mrs. Cohn, a "qualified" traditionalist is in her mid-thirties, a college graduate who is not currently employed. Her husband currently earns approximately $45,000 a year. Mrs. Cohn grew up in a neighborhood which she describes as mostly Jewish and according to her own account had mostly Jewish friends while she was growing up.[4] Mrs. Cohn remembers a fairly high level of observance in her parents' home and recalls both the presence of Jewish ritual and art objects and the discussion of Jewish topics there. While Mrs. Cohn received only minimal Jewish education, attending Sunday school for three years, she feels that her early Jewish education was a thoroughly positive experience and an important influence on her current level of Jewishness.

Dr. Dorf, a Jewish universalist, is fifty-six years old, an anesthesiologist who currently earns more than $90,000 a year. He grew up in a community where Jewish families were a minority and recalls that only about half of his childhood friends were Jewish. Jewishness was not a prominent feature of Dr. Dorf's parental home. His parents neither celebrated many Jewish rituals nor observed many Jewish customs while he was growing up. As he remembers, his parents had few Jewish ritual objects in their home and rarely discussed Jewish topics. In spite of the rather low level of Jewishness in his parental home, Dr. Dorf was sent to an afternoon Hebrew school for several years, and also received private bar mitzvah tutoring from the cantor of the local congregation. He does not, however, feel that his Jewish education was a positive or especially useful experience and does not consider it an important influence on his current pattern of Jewish practice nor a significant factor in his present attitudes on Jewish matters.

Mrs. Cohn, who grew up among and with mostly other Jews, prefers a community in which Jews are in the majority and would not react negatively if the community in which she now lives were to become virtually all Jewish. Dr. Dorf, on the other hand, would react negatively to such a development. As he sees it:

> I prefer a community with 'proportional' Jewish population. Variety enriches life; ethnic sameness is narrow, small, ghetto-like, confining, not a true picture of the real world because it's only a part of it. I think one-quarter to one-third would be about right. This is required to insure social, community, and school relationships.

Not at all surprising in the case of Dr. Dorf, but strikingly so in that of Mrs. Cohn, both express the opinion that only half or fewer of the friends of an American Jew should be Jewish. Mrs. Cohn, however, more in keeping with her own background, community preferences, and situation as a mother of young children, feels it is very important that most of her children's friends be Jewish. Dr. Dorf, while equivocating somewhat on the issue, in the end feels that it is not an especially important matter.

Neither Dr. Dorf nor Mrs. Cohn feels strongly one way or the other about Jewish day school education. When probed, however, their respective reactions reveal interesting differences. Mrs. Cohn feels that "school and religion should be separate – in order to maintain the importance and individuality of each." Dr. Dorf, by contrast, once again refers to the importance of diversity and the avoidance of narrowness: "Kids should have an opportunity to be educated in the heterogeneous society in which they must some day immerse themselves."

In light of their different backgrounds and views, fascinating patterns of similarity and contrast emerge in Dr. Dorf's and Mrs. Cohn's respective attitudes on other issues relating to Jewishness and children. Both Mrs. Cohn and Dr. Dorf would discourage the prospective intermarriage of one of their children and both feel that transmitting Jewishness to children serves as a very important motivation in their Jewish celebration.

The level of observance of Dr. Dorf, measured in terms of Hanukkah, Passover, and the lighting of Sabbath candles, is in fact a bit higher than that of Mrs. Cohn. She, however, considers Jewish law an important factor in observance while he does not. When looking for a summer camp for their children, Mrs. Cohn looks for a camp where most of the campers and staff are Jewish. Dr. Dorf, when his children were younger, chose to send them to an ethnically and religiously mixed sports camp. Mrs. Cohn, whose children are elementary school age, and Dr. Dorf, whose children are older, both have low expectations for the Jewishness of their children, though their respective hopes in this regard are somewhat higher than their expectations.

Neither Mrs. Cohn nor Dr. Dorf accepts the idea that the Jews are the chosen people. Mrs. Cohn sees anti-Semitism as a serious problem in the United States, while Dr. Dorf perceives it rather as a moderate problem.

Israel figures more prominently in Mrs. Cohn's Jewishness. She feels it is very important as both a spiritual homeland and potential place of refuge for American Jews, and is convinced that Israel's existence is essential for the continuation of Jewish life in America. While Dr. Dorf feels it is important that Israel serve as a spiritual homeland, he attributes much less significance to its potential role as a place of refuge for American Jews. Although he also feels that Israel is essential for American Jewish life, he supports this idea less enthusiastically than does Mrs. Cohn.

The attitudes of Dr. Dorf and Mrs. Cohn on the subject of "giving," despite other differences between them, are identical. Both prefer giving more to Jewish community causes and feel that while giving is both a Jewish and American value it is stressed more in Jewish culture.

Both Mrs. Cohn and Dr. Dorf see themselves as Jewish survivalists. Both are in favor of opposing intermarriage, supporting Israel, and having Jews affiliate with temples or synagogues. Mrs. Cohn, however, feels more centrally a part of and identifies more strongly with the Jewish group than does Dr. Dorf.

In regard to current residential and friendship patterns, Mrs. Cohn, who grew up in a heavily Jewish community with mostly Jewish friends and favors Jewish residential concentration, now lives in a community which she perceives having a clear majority of Jewish residents. In addition, despite her hesitance in expressing preference for Jewish associational concentration in ideal terms, Mrs. Cohn reports that most of her friends are in fact Jews.

Dr. Dorf, who grew up in a mixed community and with a mixed circle of friends, who prefers "variety" and "heterogeneity" and feels that "ethnic sameness is narrow," currently lives in a community which he describes as having "some" Jewish families. Dr. Dorf feels that ideally the friendship networks of American Jews should be fifty percent Jewish or less; in fact just over half of his current friends are Jews.

Summary and Interpretation of Profiles

A. Introduction

There are more extreme cases among the respondents than those represented by the four composite profiles. The fact that the profile characters are not dramatically distinct types representing internally consistent and mutually exclusive patterns but are rather complex constructs whose characteristics include some apparent contradictions is an accurate reflection of the complexity of the subject matter.

We should remember that the population studied was intentionally defined to minimize heterogeneity along several dimensions and thereby allow in-depth analysis of this sample of affluent, highly educated, affiliated, suburban Reform Jews.[5] A review of the four profiles will show that two basic types emerge.

On the one hand, we have Mr. Abrams, the Jewish particularist, and Mrs. Cohn, the qualified traditionalist. They represent respondents in the youngest of the three age cohorts, with relatively low educational, occupational, and income characteristics.[6] Both grew up in rather highly Jewish environments in terms of home, community, and friends, and currently live in situations of high Jewish density. The attitudes expressed by Mr. Abrams and Mrs. Cohn are, within the range of attitudes expressed in the sample, "very Jewish."

Mrs. Bloom, the Jewish survivalist, and Dr. Dorf, the Jewish universalist, on the other hand, depict respondents in the oldest of the three age cohorts, with higher educational, occupational, and income profiles. They grew up in rather less Jewish environments and currently live in situations of lower Jewish density.[7] The attitudes expressed by Mrs. Bloom and Dr. Dorf may be characterized as less positively Jewish than those of Mr. Abrams and Mrs. Cohn.

B. Points of Universal Agreement

Several points of agreement emerge across all four of the composite profiles. None of the four accepts the idea that the Jews are the chosen people and none feels strongly about Jewish day schools despite the differences which their thoughts on the matter reveal. All four are Jewish survivalists (though Mrs. Bloom is expressly labelled as such since, as is clear from her comments, Jewish survivalism is such an important cornerstone of her attitudinal array.)

Congruent with the survivalist position, all are against intermarriage, in favor of Jews giving more to support Jewish than general community causes, and consider transmission of Jewishness to their children an important motivation behind their respective patterns of Jewish celebration and observance. All more readily support the notion of Jewish associational concentration in regard to their children than for American Jews in general.

The picture which emerges from this description is one of concern with not violating the basic understandings of American society at least on an ideological level, while at the same time to varying degrees favoring those patterns of behavior which serve to insure the continuation of the Jewish group within the American setting.

The four profile characters clearly identify as Jews and want the Jewish ethnic tie to persist in the future and through their own offspring, yet frame that desire in terms acceptable in the egalitarian and pluralistic language of American public discourse. To the extent that behavioral choices may be inferred from their attitudinal preferences, they also picture the translation of that desire into reality in ways fully compatible with the freedoms and limitations of group life in the American setting, though assuming different positions within these parameters.

C. Points of Distinction

Of the four profile characters, only Mr. Abrams, the particularist, is willing to express the opinion that Jews should have mostly Jewish friends. The remaining attitudinal distinctions split the four profiles into the Abrams-Cohn - Bloom-Dorf pairings mentioned above. The former would prefer a more Jewish camp environment for their children, consider anti-Semitism a more serious problem in the United States, and feel that Israel is very important as a potential place of refuge for American Jews.

The camp-related attitude reflects more than frosting on the transmission-of-Jewishness cake. Is the summer primarily to be enjoyed as a respite from the serious business of "the year" or is the Jewish enterprise a sufficiently weighty and full-time concern to deserve attention and influence choices in matters that pertain to this potential two-month hiatus? The camp issue reflects a basic difference in the relative salience of "Jewish" and "American" within the complex interplay of components that constitute the ethnic identity of the profile characters, as do the points of distinction between the pairs regarding anti-Semitism and Israel.

Perceptions as to the seriousness of anti-Semitism fit well into a scheme in which the balance of "Jewish" and "American" is tipped to one side or the other. Respective positions regarding anti-Semitism and their consequences for different degrees of feeling "at home in" and "part of" America are as likely determinants as any of feelings about the importance of Israel as a potential refuge for American Jews.[8]

D. Apparent Paradoxes

While Dr. Dorf's parental home was rather weak Jewishly, he nonetheless received a relatively high level of Jewish education. In Mrs. Cohn's case, precisely the obverse is true: Jewishness was a more salient feature of her parental home, yet she received a relatively lower level of formal Jewish education. Further, whereas Dr. Dorf attributes little importance to his Jewish education as a factor affecting his current level of Jewishness, Mrs. Cohn considers her minimal Jewish education a very important influence on her current level of Jewishness.

A number of possible interpretations exist to account for this double discrepancy. First, the apparent reversal of the expected pattern in terms of the relation between the home environment and the amount of Jewish education received may be attributable at least in part to a different attitude towards the Jewish education of males and females. More intriguing, however, is an interpretation which relates to the role which has devolved upon formal Jewish education in the American setting.

Formal Jewish education has been called upon to fulfill a function formerly served by the family and community, namely, instilling a sense of Jewish identity, "creating" the Jewish identity of children.[9] Mrs. Cohn's parents, perhaps confident that their daughter was absorbing a sense of who she was as a Jew from the Jewish home atmosphere in which she was being raised, may have felt less urgency in encouraging any more than a minimal exposure to the Jewish classroom. Dr. Dorf's parents, perhaps realizing the lack of Jewishness they were transmitting to their young son at home, may have felt compelled to call upon the Jewish school to "make my son a Jew." The respective decisions of Mrs. Cohn's and Dr. Dorf's parents may have been further reinforced by their children's respective friendship patterns and the Jewish composition of the respective communities in which they were growing up.

Second, the reversal of the expected pattern in terms of the relation between the level of Jewish education and its later importance as an influence on Jewishness, may also be attributable to multiple factors. It might stem from the quality of the Jewish education itself, as opposed to its measurable quantity. Dr. Dorf's lower estimation of its influence may reflect the discrepancy between his relatively high level of Jewish education and his relatively low Jewish attitudinal profile. Potentially positive effects of formal Jewish schooling may, as many Jewish educators have long suspected, be dependent in the long run on reinforcement in the home. Finally, given the rather minimalist nature of the entire range of Jewish education with which we are dealing, it may be that the affective component far outweighs the cognitive in terms of lasting effects.

The other consistent reversal of the expected occurs in the matter of observance. The two characters with generally lower profiles in terms of Jewish background, density, and attitudes have relatively higher observance patterns in terms of Hanukkah, Passover, and the lighting of Sabbath candles. Here again, quantitative differences may mask more significant qualitative differences. Assuming, however, that such is not the case and that the apparent contradiction holds, we may again be faced with differences which are at least in part a function of the relative strength of other aspects of the Jewish environment.

Transmission of Jewishness to their children was cited consistently as very important by all four profile characters. Given the relatively weaker Jewish environments provided by Dr. Dorf and Mrs. Bloom, as reflected in their Jewish density and attitudinal patterns, they perhaps feel more compelled to celebrate these minimal, rather painless, and widely observed occasions in order to transmit some degree of Jewishness to their children.

E. Themes from Open-Ended Responses

A full spectrum of views emerges from the statements of the three profile characters who comment on why the proportion of Jews would make a difference in their choice of a new community.

Mr. Abrams, who prefers to live in a mostly Jewish community, responds in the most explicitly Jewish fashion. He is forthright about considering Jews "my own people." His reasons for preferring a majority of Jews fall into three categories:
1) He is most "comfortable" in a "Jewish atmosphere" which he attributes to commonality of "interests, backgrounds, beliefs." Mr. Abrams does not specify that these interests, backgrounds, or beliefs refer necessarily or even primarily to those which are classically or traditionally Jewish. It is every bit as likely that Mr. Abrams includes in his reference general characteristics such as a high level of secular education; interests which include, for example, preferences for certain types of leisure-time

pursuits; and beliefs which pertain to the nature of family, community, and the general society in which one lives.

These characteristics and attitudes – evolving from a combination of shared historical and cultural experience in interaction with the American setting – may serve as a redefinition of what is Jewish for Jews in America and function as a new basis of affinity and feelings of commonality.[10] We will see below a similar reference by Dr. Dorf, although his statement emerges from a very different perspective.

2) Mr. Abrams prefers a Jewish environment to foster and reinforce the Jewish identity and identification of his children and insure their social interaction with other Jews.

3) He sees a critical mass of Jews as necessary to "support Jewish institutions." Functionally this guarantees the existence of a Jewish community and symbolically it serves to heighten awareness that such a community exists - the "Jewish community feeling" to which Mr. Abrams refers.

Mrs. Bloom's preference is for a "mixed" community, which can translate into anywhere from equal proportions of Jews and non-Jews to a small, but noticeable Jewish minority. Mrs. Bloom's own ideal falls somewhere between these two ends of the "mixed community" spectrum. Mrs. Bloom wants to avoid a "ghetto" atmosphere and live "realistically." Her actual preference for a substantial Jewish minority in fact bears little relation to the "real" proportion of Jews in the population. She is compelled to increase the proportion of Jews in her ideal community beyond their less than three percent representation in the population "able to participate in Jewish culture" and to have a "viable Jewish community."

In addition to these ingroup factors, Mrs. Bloom stresses the importance of intergroup interaction, but again from a Jewish perspective: to be able to "be proud of Jewish identity in the face of all the others." Mrs. Bloom's own personal situation does not dictate living in a majority Jewish setting: her Jewish friendship network could remain intact despite lack of physical proximity; she is less in need of easy access to the temple – though she would still retain her membership – as her children are beyond religious school age. Though Mrs. Bloom prefers a less heavily Jewish community than Mr. Abrams, her reasoning, even in the case of intergroup relations, nonetheless derives very much from Jewish motivations.

In Dr. Dorf's argument, we see some of the same themes as in Mrs. Bloom's statement, but with a much less positive Jewish nuance. His emphasis is strongly on the pluses of "variety"; on the necessity of living in the "real world"; and on the negative implications of Jewish residential concentration, which he describes as "narrow, small, ghetto-like, confining."

Strikingly, despite this more negative posture, Dr. Dorf's definition of "proportional Jewish population" ("I think one-quarter to one-third would be about right") also greatly exaggerates Jewish representation within the general population. His reasons for preferring what is still very much a disproportionate Jewish presence, despite the major differences between Dr. Dorf and Mr. Abrams, remind us of the latter's appreciation of characteristics and attitudes which Jews have in common. Dr. Dorf wants to insure "social, community, and school relationships" – not traditional Jewish content, but rather interests and attitudes that have come to be considered characteristic of American Jews.

A range of attitudes is also afforded by the three statements on Jewish day schools in America, in spite of all three coming as comments on a position which claims to neither strongly favor nor oppose day schools.

Mr. Abrams once again offers the most positive Jewish response. While he does not favor the idea for his own children, he feels that the option of Jewish parochial education should exist for those who want it. In fact, Mr. Abrams favors the objectives of day school education. He feels, however, that these objectives are more appropriately achieved through other means, namely, family, Jewish camps, and Jewish supplementary education.

Mrs. Cohn, with some parallel to Mrs. Bloom's position regarding community composition, stresses the dimension of intergroup relations in American society. She adheres to the classic position of separation of church and state, phrasing it in terms of separation of "school and religion." Each is important to her, but as in the American credo, each in its own place and time.

Dr. Dorf, true to his preference for "variety" and avoidance of parochial "narrowness," emphasizes the importance of exposure to and experience in the "heterogeneous society" in which Jewish children will eventually live as adult Americans.

On the subject of day schools we thus have what may be seen as a middle position assumed by Mrs. Cohn which is framed on either side by a more particular and a more universalistic perspective.

Finally, we note that the expression of opposition to intermarriage in terms of difficulties in marriage is associated with relatively more Jewish background, density, and attitudes. Mr. Abrams, perhaps feeling safe to assume that the importance of Jewishness has been successfully transmitted to his children through his choice of community and friends and through the translation of his positive Jewish attitudes into a Jewish home atmosphere, chooses to emphasize the potential difficulties added to the already problematic state of marriage in modern American society. In keeping with his stress on Jewish feelings and the importance of family in transmission of Jewish identity, Mr. Abrams also mentions the ramifications of interaction with non-Jewish in-laws.

Mrs. Bloom, who apparently has not previously acted to accentuate the importance of Jewishness to her children, is suddenly faced with a situation which is threatening in terms of personal continuity. Witness her eventual gut-level reaction to the prospect of seeing her grandchildren "attend church." Her more general concern with the future of the Jewish people evolves as a direct extension of this most immediate personal threat, broadened and raised to a more abstract level. The almost instinctual aversion, however, remains clear throughout, including her dramatic statement "not to accomplish through intermarriage what Hitler failed to do in the Holocaust."

Notes

1. Mr. Abrams represents the high Jewish density category, having both mostly Jewish friends and living in a mostly Jewish community. The representative status of Mrs. Bloom, however, is potentially problematic. The mixed Jewish density category includes both those like Mrs. Bloom who have mostly Jewish friends but live in a community where Jews are the minority, and those who live in a majority Jewish community but whose friendship circle includes half or fewer Jews. As those in situations similar to Mrs. Bloom clearly predominate in the mixed Jewish density category (constituting over three-fourths of this group), it is reasonable to have Mrs. Bloom represent the mixed Jewish density category as Mr. Abrams represents the high Jewish density group.

2. All quotes in the Profiles' sections are taken from the responses to the open-ended items on the survey instrument. Each quote represents a composite of the answers of respondents holding views similar to those of the Profile character to whom they are attributed.

3. The descriptions of Mr. Abrams and Mrs. Bloom were derived from the relationships among background, density, and attitudes, with the implied causal sequence of background on density and density on attitudes. The portraits of Mrs. Cohn and Dr. Dorf reflect the implied causal sequence of background on attitudes and attitudes on density. Information on the relationship between attitudes as independent variables and density as a dependent variable was derived from the *rows* of the tables of crosstabulations of attitudinal variables by density variables.

4. The Jewish background of both Mrs. Cohn and Dr. Dorf is based on the association of Jewish background factors with attitudes found to correlate with Mrs. Cohn's and Dr. Dorf's respective general social characteristic profile.

5. See Appendix A for a description of the parameters placed on the sample population.

6. "Relative" is stressed in relation to the highly skewed nature of the sample as a whole towards the upper end of the educational, occupational, and income spectra.

7. The difference in terms of Jewish density is primarily a function of community composition. Over two-thirds of the entire sample

describe themselves as having all or mostly Jewish friends.

8. In fact, positive correlations were found between both the camp and anti-Semitism and the anti-Semitism and Israel measures.

9. In this regard it is ironic that studies of the effects of Jewish education point to the fact that family still seems to be a more important determinant of adult Jewish patterns. Harold Himmelfarb, for example, in his doctoral dissertation, "The Impact of Religious Schooling: The Effects of Jewish Education Upon Adult Religious Involvement" (University of Chicago 1974), found that: "...the general impact of Jewish schooling is an accentuation effect. Where students come to school predisposed to religious values, religious schooling accentuates those values; but where students are not so predisposed, schooling has little impact." (p.144) He also found that "Generally, Jewish schooling does not have any lasting effect until there has been a total of at least 3000 hours of such religious studies" (p.145), a total significantly higher than the number of hours an average American Jewish child spends in Jewish education. While families look to Jewish education as a surrogate agency of Jewish socialization, the evidence indicates that "Jewish schooling tends primarily to accentuate the effects of family..." (Himmelfarb, p.149).

10. Parsons refers to this phenomenon as "bridging," whereby a group develops attributes and attitudes that are both congruent with its own particular culture and valued in the host society. Though Parsons is dealing with deviant groups, some of whose critical defining characteristics differ from those of ethnic minorities, nonetheless many of the points he raises regarding the dynamics of the relationship between the subgroup and the dominant society are applicable to the situation of ethnic minorities. See Talcott Parsons, "Deviant Behavior and Social Control," *The Social System*, Glencoe, Illinois: Free Press, 1951, pp. 288-297.

CHAPTER TEN

CONCLUSIONS: THE JEWISHNESS OF SUBURBAN REFORM JEWS

The experience of the Jewish group in America has been different from that of its primarily east European forebears in several critical areas.[1] Notable among them has been the geographic freedom of Jews within the United States. The initial concentration of east European Jewish immigrants in the northeast and mid-Atlantic states was more the result of their desire for a familiar island amidst the foreignness of their new home and of the location of available work than of external hostility and discrimination.

To be sure, such prejudice and much discrimination certainly existed, related to both general anti-immigrant and specific anti-Jewish sentiment. Such attitudes were occasionally raised to the level of ideology in political platforms and certainly among fringe hate groups. Xenophobic feelings were clearly expressed in the restrictive immigration laws of the 1920's which discriminated particularly against those of eastern and southern European origins. At no point, however, were restrictions on the movement or settlement of Jewish immigrants and their descendants within the United States incorporated into the law of the land.

As they acculturated and became less dependent on ethnic enclaves for commonalities of language and customs, as improved transportation allowed workers to live farther from their place of work, these immigrant Jews and their children were increasingly free to disperse. Further dispersion for second and third generation American Jews was facilitated as they ascended the educational, occupational, and income ladders and as local restrictive housing practices were declared illegal and fell into disrepute.

Acculturation and increased contact with non-Jewish Americans in residential, educational, occupational, and civic settings similarly allowed for the potential modification of ethnically homogeneous friendship patterns. The absence of legal and legislative intervention in the realm of ethnic identity and the general openness of American society, cou-

194

pled with increasing residential and associational freedom, seemed to mean that American Jews were free to leave Jewish residential enclaves, friendship networks, and indeed the Jewish group itself.

The reality of the American Jewish experience has of course shown that Jews have by and large chosen neither to abandon their identity as members of the Jewish group nor to relinquish their largely Jewish associational networks.

The pattern of and need for continued Jewish residential concentration in particular among the Orthodox or traditionally observant segments of the American Jewish population is recognized both by those involved and by students of American Jewish life. The traditionally observant American Jew must still be able to walk to synagogue on the Sabbath and on major holidays. Less stringent geographically, but nonetheless operative – and highly symbolic – demands for residential concentration among this segment of the population arise from the continued need for kosher meat, for access to suppliers of ritual objects and religious texts, for a "good 'shomer shabbos' (observant of the Sabbath laws) bakery," and so on. A more generalized preference for living in at least a majority Jewish setting results both from these specific needs and from more diffuse social and symbolic choices. But what of the opposite end of the Jewishly-affiliated spectrum? What of American Reform Jews who no longer accept the injunction of eating kosher meat or the prohibition against driving to temple on the Sabbath and holidays? It was commonly assumed that, no longer restricted by the demands of Jewish law to live in close physical proximity to Jewish institutions and the purveyors of Jewish services on the one hand, and lured by the invitation to participate as equals in the good life of suburban America, the issue of high Jewish density would become for them a moot point.

Membership in and even regular attendance at a Reform temple dictates living only as close as the distance that can be driven in a reasonable amount of time. That venerable institution of the suburban Jewish educational system, the car pool, allows the same broad residential spread in the maintenance of that Jewish educational system. Likewise, the maintenance of Jewish friendship networks no longer necessitates a high degree of Jewish residential concentration, as the testimony ascribed to

Mrs. Bloom and the fact that only twenty percent of the sample social-
izes primarily with residents of their own community attest. And in fact,
in contradistinction to the older ideal of a community of all or nearly all
Jews, a counter ideal of the "mixed" or "balanced" community was born.

What is striking is that for Jews the preference for a "mixed" community
– ranging from a high of the "fifty-fifty" community type to a more
moderate "proportional" representation of "some" Jews – is raised to
the level of ideology. This elevation no doubt has its roots in the salience
of the identity and intergroup issues in the consciousness of American
Jews; indeed it might be said, in their preoccupation with it.

For non-Jews in America there is of course the nostalgic ideal of the old
neighborhood – in Boston, the North End and East Boston for Italians,
South Boston for the Irish. But for those who move out, the exodus is
more a matter of fact, of success making possible fulfilling the dream of
the single-family home in the suburbs.[2] While their leaving may be less
matter-of-fact for those who stay behind, nonetheless leaving for those
who move out does not become the subject of a new ideal scheme of
"mixing", "balance", "diversity", and the like.

It is, however, an ideal for the Jews of Liberty, which is perceived as less
Jewish, in fact, than demographic statistics would bear out. Liberty is,
by virtue of its colonial heritage, the perceived make-up of its population, and the tenor of the lifestyle there, the quintessentially American
community. *And the Jewish residents of Liberty consciously and explicitly want it to stay that way.* For Liberty to actually become or even
be perceived as a primarily Jewish community would negate one of the
sources of its attractiveness to the Jews who chose to move there.[3]

Over sixty percent of the Liberty residents in the sample want a community of only "some or few" Jews; a bit over thirty-five percent would
prefer the upper limit of the mixed community, with Jews constituting
about half of the population; but *less than one percent* of the respondents
who live in Liberty want a community that is "all or mostly" Jewish. The
proportion of Jews and non-Jews in Liberty, perceived by almost ninety
percent of Liberty respondents as including only "some" Jews, was a positive factor for almost two-thirds of them in choosing to live there. Over

three-fourths of Liberty respondents would react negatively were their community to become an all or almost all Jewish suburb. Were they to move again, less than one-third of these respondents would regard a community of even "half or more" Jews as ideal.

We should of course not lose sight of the fact that, despite the ideal of minority Jewish representation in the community and of the "mixed" community itself, the respondents living in Liberty are institutionally affiliated with the local Jewish community and in fact identify rather strongly with the Jewish group, their aversion to Jewish particularism notwithstanding.

The discussion thus far has dealt with the ideal of the "mixed" community and with the assumption that high Jewish residential concentration is no longer critical among other than traditionally observant Jews. What light do the findings of this study have to shed on the opposite position?

There is in the sample another group of respondents living in a different situation of Jewish residential concentration, though they too are suburban Reform American Jews. Nearly ninety percent of the respondents who are Newington residents and members of Temple Tikvah perceive of their community as being at least half Jewish and *over ninety percent want it that way.* More than three-fourths of these respondents cited this high proportion of Jews as a positive factor in their choice of their present community, and a similar proportion would regard half or more Jews as the ideal in choosing a new community were they to move.

In fact, Newington is perceived as more Jewish than it is based solely on the actual percentage of Jews in its population.[4] Its Jewish character is reinforced by the presence of numerous Jewish institutions: Orthodox, Conservative, and Reform congregations, kosher butcher shops, Jewish bakeries, and even a Jewish mayor. The perception of Newington as a Jewish community is facilitated by its being divided into several "villages" with some particularly known as Jewish areas. Its symbolic importance as a Jewish community is enhanced by its being one of the two principal and prestigious areas of third-settlement[5] for Jews, one of two communities to absorb Jews at a particular period of their migration out from the city proper. Among those moving into the Boston area, Newington is still a preferred choice of middle and upper-middle class Jews who want to live in a clearly Jewish community.

Thus, for the members of Temple Tikvah in the sample, Reform and suburban though they be, the preference for high Jewish residential concentration is very much alive. Indeed for both Tikvah and Am Shalom members, though falling on opposite sides of the Jewish residential concentration fence in terms of both their perceptions of place of residence and attitude towards residential concentration, the issue of Jewish residential concentration is far from a moot point.

Is perceived Jewish density in fact associated with a difference in attitudes? The answer, based on the findings of this study, is a resounding yes. If we look at those with the "least Jewish" attitudes in this sample of affiliated Reform Jews, we find almost uniformly that they are both living in situations of lower Jewish residential concentration and have a lower proportion of Jews among their friends.

Findings presented previously reveal that there is a positive association between low current Jewish density and the "least Jewish" attitudes on all five of the major components of the particularism factor (reaction to community becoming an all Jewish suburb; desired community composition: proportion of Jews; proportion of friends of an American Jew should be Jewish; importance that most of children's friends be Jewish; and attitudes towards Jewish day schools in America). This applies as well to all four of the measures of group belonging and identification (identification with the Jewish group; good Jewish education: strengthening commitment to the Jewish people; survival; and in-group feelings). Low current Jewish density is likewise associated with "least Jewish" attitudes for both the affective and behavioral reactions to intermarriage, and for selection of a hypothetical camp for one's children.

In addition, "least Jewish" attitudes on all six of the Israel variables (essentiality of Israel for American Jewish life; good Jewish education: developing a strong feeling for Israel; importance of Israel as a spiritual homeland, center for Jewish culture, refuge for Jews in distress, potential refuge for American Jews) are associated specifically with low Jewish residential concentration. This holds as well for the attitudes towards giving, and for lesser perceptions as to the seriousness of anti-Semitism. "Least Jewish" positions on hopes for the Jewishness of children, on attitudes towards chosenness, and in level of observance are similarly associated with low Jewish associational concentration.[6]

Moreover, from the multiple classification analyses,[7] we note the high correlation of current Jewish density in a monotonic relationship with the Particularism Scale, the Intermarriage scale, attitudes towards a Jewish camp setting, the Belonging and Identification Scale, and the attitude towards giving. In seven of the ten measures tested, the highest position on the dependent attitudinal variable was held by those in the high Jewish density category and the lowest position by those in the low Jewish density category.

A high level of educational attainment and occupational prestige were associated with low current Jewish density, as was low background Jewish density. Background Jewish density and education were shown in the multiple classification analysis as well to be highly correlated with Jewish density. Background Jewish density was positively related to current Jewish density, while education was inversely related to current Jewish density.

High education, occupation, and relatively high income were generally associated with less Jewish attitudes, as were low background Jewish density, low levels of parental observance and Jewish content in the parental home, and low estimations of the importance of one's Jewish education as a factor affecting current levels of Jewishness. Further, in this context of the relationship between background and attitudes, the multiple classification analysis points to: a strong correlation of education and attitudes towards camp, anti-Semitism, particularism, and the Belonging and Identification Scale, with high education associated with less Jewish attitudes on these measures; and an association of low background Jewish density with lower positions on the Particularism, Belonging and Identification, and Israel scales, and on the attitudes towards camp. The association of background Jewish density with attitudes appears for the most part to be mediated through its effect on current Jewish density.

High current Jewish density, then, is associated with more positive Jewish attitudes. A relatively fuller Jewish background is also associated indirectly with more positive Jewish attitudes and directly with high current Jewish density. A relatively higher level of secular education and occupational prestige are associated with both less Jewish attitudes and low current Jewish density. These associations are summarized in the chart below.[8]

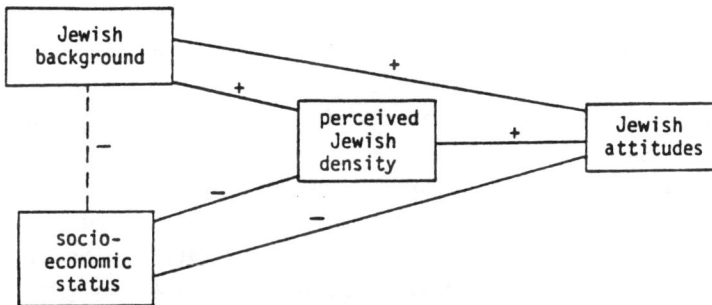

This complex of relationships highlights the critical importance of continued Jewish residential and associational concentration[9] for the maintenance of strong Jewish ethnicity even in the suburban setting and among a less traditional segment of the American Jewish population. These findings confirm what Yancey, Ericksen, and Juliani put forth as probable: It is possible...for ethnic networks to exist in geographically dispersed groups, yet the effect of ethnicity may be strongest among members who are geographically clustered.[10]

Despite being the largest Jewish community in the world, American Jewry comprises a very small proportion of the general American population. In demographic terms, American Jews, constituting only around 2.6% of the population of the United States, may be considered a rare population. Further, American Jews have neither a history of legally enforced segregation nor are they characterized by immutable differentiating racial characteristics.

While Jews have not scattered randomly among the American populace, they have spread across virtually all of the United States. German Jewish immigrants of the nineteenth century were known for their westward movement throughout much of what was then the American frontier.

Later Jewish immigrants from eastern Europe, also entering the United States almost exclusively through the ports of the Northeast, tended at first to remain concentrated in these cities. They too, however, and especially their descendants later spread across the continent. Witness the fact that the second largest Jewish community in America, Los Angeles, is located on the west coast. Miami, which recently became the third largest, is in (though maybe not "part of") the South. Chicago, the fourth largest, is in the north central United States.

In theory, Jews are free to disperse within the American population. Their mobility is not restricted legally nor much impeded by discrimination. Neither is the vast majority of American Jewry dependent any longer on ethnic enclaves in terms of language or the procurement of traditional Jewish services. Nonetheless, only in New York City could Jews scatter randomly and still maintain a degree of Jewish concentration. And, given the miniscule representation of Jews in the American population, unless so concentrated, the potential for Jewish group cohesion would be significantly reduced with the loss of one of its primary structural supports.[11]

In the greater Boston area, also one of the ten largest Jewish communities in the United States, Jews have in fact moved south, west, and north of the city. Within these axes of movement, however, they need concentration or they face the prospect of becoming invisible. Given the complex of relationships revealed in this study, if the Jewish factor does not continue to serve as a critical consideration in where Jews move, the future strength of Jewish ethnicity is called into serious question.

This is especially true as Jews continue to move towards higher levels of secular education which is itself associated with lower Jewish density and with less Jewish attitudes. In terms of transmission of Jewish ethnicity to the next generation, the critical nature of the maintenance of Jewish density is further reinforced as high background Jewish density is associated both directly with high current Jewish density and indirectly with higher positions on measures of Jewish attitudes.

Thus the effects of ethnic "clustering," to use Yancey, Ericksen, and Juliani's term, can be seen not only as consequences of high Jewish density, but over time also become antecedents of future ethnic clustering. The Jewish density of the current generation is by definition the background Jewish density of the next generation.

The early prediction advanced primarily by the adherents of the Chicago environmentalist school has clearly not come to pass. Jews continue to exist in America well beyond their exodus from ethnically homogeneous ghettos. Given the interplay of structural and cultural correlates of Jewish ethnicity which emerges in this research, the recent emphasis on structural conditions as critical supports of ethnicity provides a much needed balance to the earlier almost exclusive focus on cultural dynamics.

It is, however, the combination of both the structural and cultural foci – and not the structural emphasis alone – which yields the most comprehensive picture of Jewish ethnicity in the United States. It is this combined focus on both the structural and cultural correlates of ethnicity which is the most appropriate framework within which to study the ethnicity of American Jews.

Evolving within the context of this theoretical framework, what light do the findings of the present research have to shed on the central issues posed at the outset of this study?

Is Jewishness still a factor in critical behavioral decisions among well-educated, affluent, acculturated American Jews living in an open society? For such a population, who experience very few restrictions on their residential and friendship choices, is the Jewish dimension brought to bear on questions of where and among whom they choose to live and with whom they choose to associate?

We have noted the positive association of Jewish background and especially of having grown up in a highly Jewish community with both currently living in a highly Jewish community and with expressing preference for the same. Similarly, we have noted the strong association of having grown up in a highly Jewish friendship network with currently having a high proportion of Jewish friends, despite the reluctance to express this preference other than in relation to one's children.

Jewishness alone may not be the most salient factor in choice of community. Nonetheless, Jewish background, especially background Jewish residential concentration, is a critical factor associated with choosing a more Jewish community from among otherwise equally attractive alternatives. As we have seen, what is further striking in the case of those who opt for less Jewish communities is that this preference is raised to the level of ideology – the preference for a "mixed", "balanced", "diversified" community.

As in the case of community but to a somewhat lesser extent, Jewish background, especially background associational concentration, is a critical factor associated with choosing a higher proportion of Jewish friends from among a pool of those who are otherwise eligible in terms of commonalities of general background and current social class characteristics. As noted, however, even those who choose mostly Jewish friends do not say that they prefer mostly Jewish friends, as such expression is seen as unacceptable in an egalitarian American setting. They do, nonetheless, express their preference that their children have mostly Jewish friends, as transmission of Jewishness and continuity are issues of such critical concern.

For such a population, are differences in residential and associational patterns associated with different attitudes in matters that relate centrally to Jewish ethnicity? If so, which aspects of such attitudinal sets are most strongly associated with residential and associational patterns?

While the findings of this cross-sectional study do not allow us to conclude that attitudes are *affected* by Jewish density, they do clearly demonstrate that higher current Jewish density is strongly *associated* with more Jewish attitudes.[12] This is especially true of attitudes pertaining to identification with the group, distinction between group members and outsiders, and group maintenance and continuity.

Stronger objection and opposition to intermarriage and preference for a more Jewish camp setting for one's children are part of the attitudinal complex positively associated with high Jewish density, particularly as transmission to the next generation is seen as critical for group maintenance and continuity. A higher evaluation of the seriousness of anti-

Semitism may been seen as accompanying the heightened distinction between "us" and "them." Emphasis on the importance of Israel's potential roles and essentiality for American Jewish life relates both to the self-conception of a strong "us," as well as to a central expression of the shared cultural heritage of the group. More Jewish attitudes in regard to giving are supportive of what is itself seen as a supportive institutional structure.

Are differences in Jewish background related to differences in Jewish attitudes? Is Jewish background associated with differences later in life among highly educated, affluent, acculturated Jews in terms of attitudes along dimensions that relate centrally to Jewish ethnicity?

The findings indicate that while Jewish background, especially in the form of background Jewish density, is positively associated with more Jewish attitudes, the major portion of this association appears to be mediated through the strong positive association of Jewish background and current Jewish density.

The associations highlighted above are maintained even when controls for socioeconomic status are introduced. Secular education, however – to the extent that it varies in this generally very highly educated population – appears to function as a confounding factor, with a high level of educational attainment associated with more universalistic attitudes and behavior. Since age – within the age range available in this sample – does not function as such a factor, we can point to a degree of stability in these relationships over time.

These factors, then, are among the structural and cultural correlates of Jewish ethnicity. Both their recognition and especially the pattern of their association is significant. Jewish background and Jewish density are still, in the last quarter of the twentieth century, critical factors among highly educated, affluent, acculturated Reform Jews living – in Yancey, Ericksen, and Juliani's phrase – in the "quasi communities" of suburban America. The structural and cultural components of Jewish ethnicity continue to be intricately related even in the case of the particular population surveyed, in regard to which the disassociation of these two elements has been widely posited.

The recent structural emphasis in the study of ethnic group maintenance is supported in findings that Jewish density is still very much a distinguishing factor within this research population. The need to combine this structural emphasis with continued attention to the cultural correlates of these structural factors is demonstrated in findings which indicate that differences in Jewish density are clearly associated with different sets of attitudinal clusters.

While Jewish background is usually included in studies of all segments of American Jewry, Jewish density, as indicated earlier in this chapter, has generally not been considered important in relation to other than traditional Jewish populations. The positive association between Jewish density and a broad range of attitudinal measures suggests that Jewish density must be included as a critical variable in future studies of the ethnicity of American Jews.

The sociological literature on ethnicity has in a sense come full circle since the beginning of the twentieth century. Originating in the structural emphasis of the Chicago school, the treatment of ethnicity was dominated during an extended period by the primarily cultural focus of the melting pot and cultural pluralism theorists. This emphasis has in turn recently given way to a reemergence of a structural focus. The strong positive association between Jewish density and Jewish attitudes highlights the importance of adequate consideration of both the structural and cultural correlates of ethnicity and of the interaction between these structural and cultural factors. This conceptual synthesis emerges as the suggested basis of future research on ethnic groups in American society.

A final question of course remains as to the specific future of the Jewish group in that society. While this study has dealt directly with suburban Jews affiliated with Reform temples, this population may represent a vanguard among American Jews in terms of both its residential location and its social characteristic profile.

Such populations have frequently been considered vanguard elements in the assimilatory process as well. In this context, Jewish density was found to be positively associated with significant attitudinal differences between the two communities studied. However, while those respondents living in situations of high Jewish density tend to hold attitudes more supportive of Jewish ethnicity, within this sample of temple-affiliated Jews those respondents living in situations of lower Jewish density were nonetheless also found to be strongly identified as Jews.

They have in fact successfully undertaken the somewhat surprising task of creating an active Jewish community in the midst of an archetypically American suburb. Having "made it" in American society, able "at last" to be simply "Americans" without a hyphen, they have nonetheless chosen to maintain and affirm their identity as American Jews, though doing so in a manner different from that of more traditional Jewish populations. This finding suggests a reconsideration of the implications of acculturation for Jews in a modern, open society and perhaps even a redefinition of what it means to be a Jew in such a setting.

Notes

1. For an elaboration of some of these differences and their implications, see Ben Halpern, "America Is Different" in Marshall Sklare, ed., *The Jews*, Glencoe, Illinois: The Free Press, 1958, pp. 23-39.
2. Recent difficulties in realizing this dream must of course be mentioned, as must the newer trend towards residence in rehabilitated inner-city areas, the "gentrification" of old ethnic neighborhoods.
3. This is certainly true for the respondents and in all likelihood even more so for the less identified or non-affiliated Jews of Liberty.
4. Interestingly, the perception of Newington as more Jewish than it really is, is paralleled by its being known as more affluent than it really is. The general perception of Newington is derived from a focus on a few of its sub-areas, while other, working-class sections are generally overlooked.
5. The "West End" was the principal area of first-settlement for the Jews of Boston; Roxbury, Dorchester, and later Mattapan the principal areas of second-settlement. More recently Jews have moved to several communities west and south of Boston, in addition to a long-standing concentration of Jews on the North Shore.
6. Some of the "least Jewish" positions were associated inversely with both the combined measure for Jewish density and both of its components, and others with the combined measure and one component, or with both components. For the sake of succinctness of presentation, only one such relationship was cited above for each set of attitudinal measures. Exceptions to the general pattern of association, while few and previously discussed, should again be mentioned: low observance and a lower position on the threat-to-Judaism expression of opposition to intermarriage were associated with high residential concentration. The latter attitudinal measure was also associated with high associational concentration.
7. References to the multiple classification analysis cite adjusted scores.
8. The relationship between Jewish background and socioeconomic status is denoted by a broken line as it was not explicitly dealt with in the course of this study. Since the relationship between Jewish background and current Jewish density and Jewish attitudes is positive while that between socioeconomic status and current Jewish density and Jewish attitudes is inverse, logic demands that the re-

lationship between Jewish background and socioeconomic status also be inverse. When crosstabulations of Jewish background and socioeconomic status variables were run, such in fact proved generally to be the case.

9. The component of residential concentration was stressed over that of associational concentration in the introductory pages of this chapter as the former seems to be more at issue: while the respondents display a range of variation in terms of current Jewish residential concentration, approximately 70% of the entire sample – including almost 60% of the Am Shalom respondents – nonetheless claim to have mostly Jewish friends.

10. Yancey, Ericksen, and Juliani, op. cit., p. 400.

11. Erich Rosenthal, in one of his well-known studies of Jewish intermarriage, concludes: "Students of Jewish life in America have repeatedly observed that the size of the local Jewish community is a significant factor in the survival of the Jewish group. The larger the Jewish community, the easier it is to organize communal activities, to effect the voluntary concentration of Jewish families in specific residential neighborhoods, and to maintain an organized marriage market. Conversely, the smaller the local community, the more difficult it becomes to maintain an organized community and marriage market." (Erich Rosenthal, "Jewish Intermarriage in Indiana," *American Jewish Year Book*, 68 (1967): 243-264).

12. The consistently strong positive association which emerged between Jewish density and attitudes recommends further investigation of Jewish density as an independent variable among other segments of American Jewry. As a preliminary step in this direction, associations were analyzed between a parallel measure of Jewish density and eleven attitudinal variables using the original data from the 1975 study of greater Boston Jewry. These associations were examined for three subgroups in the 1975 sample: members of Conservative temples, members of Reform temples, and respondents who were not currently affiliated with a temple or synagogue. As in the present study, only those who were currently married and who had children under eighteen years of age living at home were included in the analysis.

The attitudinal variables tested included preference for a Jewish neighborhood and Jewish friends, identification with the Jewish group, and attitudes towards Israel, intermarriage, anti-Semitism, and giving. The parallels with the present study are obvious. While comparison with other samples was not a central purpose of the present research, the survey instrument was nonetheless intentionally designed to facilitate comparison with the 1975 Boston study. The latter was chosen as it is a particularly well-designed and carefully executed study of Jews in the same geographical area as that from which the current sample was drawn.

Jewish density was positively associated with more Jewish attitudes on thirty of the total of thirty-three associations examined. In terms of the analysis by subgroups, Jewish density was positively associated with more Jewish attitudes on ten of the eleven attitudinal variables analyzed for each group. Thus for Conservative temple members, non-temple-members, and for an additional sample of Reform temple members, Jewish density proves, as in the present study, to be a powerful independent variable in terms of its positive association with Jewish attitudes.

APPENDICES

Appendix A: The Survey

After selecting the two temple populations to be studied, the cooperation of the respective rabbis and governing boards was secured as one of a number of steps taken to maximize response rates.

Work on the questionnaire extended through a lengthy process of refinement and revision. Pretests were carried out and the questionnaire (Appendix C) mailed after revisions based on pretest reactions.

The sampling frame was drawn from lists of the entire membership (by household) of both temples. These membership lists were screened to eliminate the following categories of people: 1) those with no minor children living at home, 2) single parent families, and 3) those not living in the community in which the temple to which they belonged was located.

Those living outside of the temple community were eliminated in order to maintain clarity in the communal base of the study and to avoid confusing the issue of residential concentration by the inclusion of respondents residing in several peripheral communities with varying concentrations of Jews. Only intact families with minor children living at home were included in order to minimize potential variation in the sample related to factors extraneous to the central analytic concerns of this study.[1]

A total of 447 eligible households remained, from which a two-thirds random sample of households was drawn, yielding a total sample of 298. Within this list of sample units, selection of actual respondents was done by starting at a randomly selected point and alternately designating either the male or the female spouse as the respondent.

Seven weeks after the initial mailing, the response rate reached 80%, a total of 238 completed responses.[2]

210

Notes

1. Despite this screening, the final sample did include one widow and two respondents who were currently divorced or separated, as well as thirty-six respondents with no minor children living at home.

Those with no minor children living at home represented 20% of the total Am Shalom membership and 17% of the total Tikvah membership. Single parent families were 8% of the total Am Shalom membership and 11% of the Tikvah total membership. Those not living in the community in which their temple was located were 16% of the total Am Shalom membership and 19% of the total Tikvah membership.

2. By temple, the number and percentage of responses were as follows: Temple Am Shalom, 129 of 158 or 81.6%; Temple Tikvah, 109 of 139 or 78.4%.

Appendix B: A Note on Tables and Statistical Procedures

Tables of crosstabulations present percentages (carried to one decimal point) for each cell. Immediately below each column are column totals which include the N for that column and the percentage of the total which that column N represents. N's for each cell can be determined by simply multiplying the percentage in a given cell by the total N for the column in which it appears. The total number of cases for each crosstabulation appears at the bottom right of each table. Independent variables follow the word "BY" in the table heading and appear across the top of the table; dependent variables precede the word "BY" and appear on the left of the table.

Gammas are reported for the crosstabulations in Chapters Four through Seven which deal directly with analysis of data according to the analytic framework which underpins this research (Chapter One, Section III, part B). Gamma was chosen as the preferred measure of association for a relatively small sample and for tables with a limited number of cells as it is not affected by tied pairs.

Together with the crosstabulations, three additional statistical procedures were utilized to form the quantitative basis for this study. In several instances, a single scale was constructed from the combined responses on a number of separate questionnaire items. This procedure was executed on the data to facilitate ease of handling and presentation, allowing the crosstabulation of one dependent by one independent variable to depict the association between a number of distinct but related measures.

Factor analyses were used to determine common underlying statistical patterns among a large number of separate variables. The statistical clusters of variables which emerged were examined to determine whether the variables which clustered statistically on each factor were also associated in terms of content. When both statistical and thematic association overlapped, those factors which were centrally related to the theoretical basis of this study were then utilized for further investigation.

Finally, multiple classification analysis was used in designing the statistical summary of findings (Chapter Eight). This procedure was chosen for its power to generate data which yield clear and concise interpretations of the nature, strength, and direction of association between variables, both independent of and controlled for the effects of other intervening dimensions.

This last point is critical. Research which employs bivariate analysis only may include findings based on spurious relationships. The use of multivariate analysis allows for control of intervening factors. For example, one theoretical position maintains that an increase in the level of secular education is associated with movement beyond the parameters of the group of origin. Jews with a very high level of secular education would thus be expected to have more contact with non-Jews, espouse more universalistic and less parochial attitudes, and be less strongly identified with the Jewish group. Does this association hold controlling for the effects of Jewish background? Does it hold controlling for the effects of current Jewish density? Alternatively, would findings revealing a strong association between Jewish background, current Jewish density, and attitudes remain intact when controlled for the effects of secular education? Multivariate analysis allows us to address such questions.

Appendix C: The Questionnaire

B R A N D E I S   U N I V E R S I T Y

Center for Modern Jewish Studies

This questionnaire is a major focus of research we are conducting on American Jews. Please answer all questions. If you are unsure of any information asked for about your spouse or your spouse's family, please give your best estimate.

Your answers will be held in strict confidence and will be used for statistical purposes only. Your effort is greatly appreciated.

Gerald L. Showstack
Study Director

First I would like to ask some questions about your background.

1. Were you born in the United States?........................___yes ___no

   Were your parents born in the U.S.?........father.........___yes ___no
   mother.........___yes ___no

   Were any of your grandparents born in the U.S.?...........___yes→ How many?____
   ___no

2. Was your spouse born in the United States?................___yes ___no

   Were your spouse's parents born in the U.S.? father.......___yes ___no
   mother.......___yes ___no

   Were any of your spouse's grandparents born in the U.S.? ___yes→ How many?____
   ___no

3. Sex: ___male ___female

4. Current marital status:
   (check one)
   ___married
   ___widowed
   ___divorced or separated
   ___never married

5. Do you have any children below age 18 living at home with you?
   ___yes→ How many?_____. What ages? /___/___/___/___/___/
   ___no   1st 2nd 3rd 4th 5th child

6. In what year were you born? ...... 19 __ __ .

   In what year was your spouse born? 19 __ __ .

7. What is your occupation and that of your spouse?

	type of work/job	self-employed	not self-employed	full-time	part-time
self					
spouse					

8. Please check the highest level of education attained by
yourself and your spouse:

a. yourself   b. your spouse

        ____completed high school or less..____
        ____some college ....____
        ____completed college ....____
        ____some graduate study............____
        ____graduate or professional degree____

9. Were you born Jewish?

___yes   ___no ⇘ Have you converted to Judaism..................___yes   ___no
  ↓   ↘ Do you currently identify as a Jew?...........___yes   ___no

Was your spouse born Jewish?

___yes   ·_no → Has your spouse converted to Judaism?.........___yes   ___no
                 ↘ Does your spouse currently identify as a Jew? ___yes   ___no

Now I would like to ask you a few questions on the subject of community.

1. What was the proportion of Jews in the community in which you grew up?
   (the town or section of the city in which you lived the most years
   between the ages of 8 to 18)?

   ___all ___most ___about half ___some ___none

2. How many years have you lived in your present
   community (that is, in Lexington or in Newton)? _____

3. What proportion of the residents of your present community are Jewish?

   ___all ___most ___about half ___some ___few

4. If you had your choice, would you like there to be more people who are Jewish in your community, less, or would you like it to be about the same as it is now?

___more   ___about the same   ___less

5. What role, if any, did <u>each</u> of the following play in your choice of your present community?

	positive role	no role at all	negative role
quality of public schools	___	___	___
proportion of Jews and non-Jews.....	___	___	___
convenience of commute to work......	___	___	___
the Jewish community or temple......	___	___	___
general attractiveness of area	___	___	___
relations of Jews and non-Jews there	___	___	___
price of homes/rental	___	___	___

Of the above factors, which are the <u>two</u> most important ones?

_____

_____

6. Consider the possibility of your community becoming an all or almost all Jewish suburb. How would you react?

___positively   ___would make no difference   ___negatively

7. If you were to move within the next year, would the proportion of Jewish families be a factor in choosing a new community in which to live?

___no   ___yes → What proportion of Jews would you regard as ideal?

___most   ___about half   ___some   ___few

Why is that? _____

_____

Now I would like to ask you some questions on the subject of friends.

1. What proportion of your friends are Jewish?

___all   ___most   ___about half   ___some   ___none

2. Are any of your non-Jewish friends married to Jews?

   ___yes → About how many? ___all   ___most   ___about half   ___some
   ___no
   ___does not apply, I have no non-Jewish friends

3. My <u>closest</u> friend is:

   (check one)
   ___Protestant
   ___Catholic
   ___Jewish
   ___other
   ___don't know his/her religion

4. To what extent do Jewish interests and occasions figure in your interacting with your Jewish friends?

   ___to a large extent
   ___to some extent
   ___to little extent
   ___not at all

5. How important is it to <u>you</u> that most of your children's friends be Jewish?

   ___extremely important
   ___very important
   ___important
   ___fairly unimportant
   ___unimportant

6. To what extent do you tend to socialize with people from each of the following categories?

	to a great extent	to some extent	to little extent	not at all
members of your temple........				
residents of your community...				

7. In general, how would you describe your relations with non-Jews?

   (check one)
   ___close friends
   ___friends
   ___acquaintances
   ___formal contacts only
   ___little contact

8. When you were growing up, how many of your friends were Jewish?

   ___all   ___most   ___about half   ___some   ___none

9. In your opinion, what proportion of the friends of an American Jew should be Jewish?

___all ___most ___about half ___some ___few ___doesn't matter

Now I would like to ask you some questions about various institutions and organizations.

1. How many years have you belonged to your present temple? _____

2. There are a variety of reasons why people join a temple. What are the three most important reasons why you joined your temple?

   a._____

   b._____

   c._____ .

3. How often do you attend services? How often does your spouse attend?

yourself		your spouse
_____	once a week or more..	_____
_____	a few times a month..	_____
_____	every few months.....	_____
_____	on High Holidays only	_____
_____	never or almost never	_____

4. During the past twelve months, how often have you participated in each of the following temple activities?

	3 times or more	once or twice	not at all
adult education classes........	_____	_____	_____
brotherhood/sisterhood.........	_____	_____	_____
conference with rabbi..........	_____	_____	_____
committee/board meeting........	_____	_____	_____
social program/affair..........	_____	_____	_____
other, specify_____	_____	_____	

5. The giving of charity is:

(check one)
___an obligation
___desirable
___optional

6. Do you think that Jews should give more to Jewish or more to general community causes, or the same to both?

___more to Jewish
___more to general
___same to both

7. Supporting worthy causes is both a Jewish and an American value. For you, is it more a Jewish value, more an American value, or equally Jewish and American?
___more a Jewish value
___more an American value
___equally Jewish and American

8. Suppose you had a thousand dollars to donate to worthy causes. How would you divide it among the following (You needn't give to all - select only those you would choose to support. Please make sure the total comes to $1000):

_____your temple
_____other local Jewish needs and institutions
_____Israel
_____United Way (Red Feather)
_____medical research (Cancer Society, Heart Assoc., and the like)
_____political causes/political parties
_____other, specify_____

Now I would like to ask your opinion on several issues.

1. Do you feel that Jews are a force in American politics? ___yes ___no

   Do you feel that Jews should be a force in American politics?

   ___yes → What kind of a force should they be? (check one)
                                        _____radical
   ___no   _____liberal
                                        _____middle-of-the-road
                                        _____conservative

2. In your opinion, how much of a problem is anti-Semitism in the United States?
   ___an extremely serious problem
   ___a fairly serious problem
   ___a moderate problem
   ___not a problem at all

3. If a child of yours were to consider marrying a non-Jew:
   a. how would you most likely feel about it?
      ___very negative
      ___somewhat negative
      ___would make no difference at all
      ___positive

      Why would you feel this way? _____

      _____

   b. which would you most likely do?
      ___strongly oppose it
      ___discourage it
      ___be neutral
      ___wouldn't mind
      ___accept it

4. In your opinion, are the Jews the chosen people?

___yes → What do you mean by that? _____

___no _____

5. To what extent do you agree with each of the following statements?

	strongly agree	agree	disagree	strongly disagree
I feel closer to other Jews than to other Americans	_____	_____	_____	_____
I feel a greater sense of responsibility to other Jews than to other Americans	_____	_____	_____	_____
When I hear someone make a negative comment about Jews in general, I usually do not take any personal offense	_____	_____	_____	_____
Being a Jew makes a difference in almost everything I do	_____	_____	_____	_____
Sometimes my view as a Jew and my view as an American conflict on important issues..	_____	_____	_____	_____
The existence of Israel is essential for the continuation of American Jewish life......	_____	_____	_____	_____

6. In your opinion, how important is it that Israel be each of the following:

	very important	important	unimportant
a spiritual homeland for the Jewish people...	_____	_____	_____
a world center for Jewish culture............	_____	_____	_____
a place of refuge for Jews in distress.......	_____	_____	_____
a potential place of refuge for American Jews	_____	_____	_____

7. Have you ever been to Israel?

___yes → How much time have you spent there altogether?_____
___no

8. In your opinion, for a Jew to be considered a good Jew, which of the
following are <u>essential</u> that s/he do? Which are <u>desirable</u>? Which
<u>make no difference</u>? Which are <u>essential not to do?</u>

	essential	desirable	makes no difference	essential not to do
accept being a Jew and not try to hide it....				
support Israel...............................				
belong to a synagogue or temple..............				
lead an ethical and moral life				
be well versed in Jewish history and culture.				
have mostly Jewish friends...................				
give Jewish candidates for political office preference................................				
be a liberal on political and economic issues				
marry within the Jewish faith................				
believe in God...............................				

9. To what extent do you agree with each of the following statements:

	strongly agree	agree	disagree	strongly disagree
Jews should support busing to achieve school integration................................				
Colleges should encourage recruitment of members of underprivileged minorities......				
Women should be given preferred treatment in hiring to make up for past discrimination..				
Increasing political conservatism on the part of Jews is an appropriate reaction to recent developments in American society....				

10. Jews have been described as an ethnic group, a religious group, a cultural
group, and a minority group. In your opinion, which are they <u>primarily</u>?

(check <u>one</u>)
___an ethnic group
___a religious group
___a cultural group
___a minority group

Please explain why you chose the answer you did._____

_____

_____

Now I would like to ask some questions about various customs and observances.

1. Do you light candles on Chanukah?

___always   ___usually   ___sometimes   ___never

2. Do you celebrate Christmas in any of the following ways?

(check as many as apply)
___have festive meal
___send Christmas cards
___share in celebrations of non-Jewish friends/neighbors
___attend Christmas service
___have lights or decorations at home
___have tree at home
___no, don't celebrate Christmas in any way

3. Do you attend a Passover seder?

___always   ___usually   ___sometimes   ___never

Do you ever have a Passover seder in your own home?
___no   ___yes → Which of the following do you do at such a seder?
(check as many as apply)
___serve matzah
___read portions of the Haggadah
___have traditional Passover plate with ritual foods
___read entire Haggadah
___sing traditional Passover songs

How important is each of the following in terms of what Passover means to you?

	very important	important	not especially important
a celebration of religious freedom......	_____	_____	_____
a celebration of the birth/independence of the Jewish people.................	_____	_____	_____
a celebration of the miracles of the exodus from Egypt....................	_____	_____	_____
a celebration which provides the occasion for a family gathering......	_____	_____	_____

4. Do you separate milk and meat at meals in your home?
___strictly   ___for the most part   ___somewhat   ___no

5. Do you regularly observe the Sabbath in any of the following ways?
(check as many as apply)
___light candles
___eat festive meal
___attend services
___say kiddush
___family time together
___no, don't observe in any way

6. Over the course of the past five years, has your observance of Jewish ritual and customs increased, decreased, or remained about the same?

___increased   ___decreased   ___remained the same

most ⟵――――⟶ least

7. Please rate your own family's level of observance of Jewish ritual and customs... | 5 | 4 | 3 | 2 | 1 | 0 | your family

Please rate that of your parents while you were growing up................ | 5 | 4 | 3 | 2 | 1 | 0 | your parents

Please rate that of your spouse's parents while s/he was growing up........ | 5 | 4 | 3 | 2 | 1 | 0 | spouse's parents

most ⟵――――⟶ least

8. How important is each of the following in terms of why you celebrate Jewish holidays or observe Jewish customs?

	very important	important	not especially important
it's part of Jewish law, commandments			
it's part of Jewish tradition, culture			
to feel part of the Jewish community			
to transmit Jewishness to my children			
to please parents or grandparents....			
to please my spouse.................			
for the general values they represent			
all Americans should preserve the culture of their own group.........			

Finally, I would like to ask some questions about Jewish education and your Jewish background.

1. Please describe your own Jewish education, that of your spouse, and the Jewish education your would ideally want for your children:

	kind of school/course	# of years
self		
spouse		
ideal for children		

2. In your opinion, how important is each of the following in
   a good Jewish education?

	very important	important	not especially important
teaching children traditional observances......	___	___	___
helping children develop their own Jewish religious beliefs and principles.............	___	___	___
developing a strong feeling for Israel.........	___	___	___
strengthening commitment to the Jewish people..	___	___	___
developing a strong defense against anti-Semitism	___	___	___
teaching children general moral values.........	___	___	___

3. In addition to Orthodox day schools (all-day education under Jewish auspices,
   with half the day spent in regular school subjects and half the day in Jewish
   studies) there is now a network of Conservative day schools and the beginnings
   of a Reform day school movement. How do you feel about the idea of Jewish day
   schools in America?

   ___strongly favor
   ___favor
   ___don't feel strongly one way or the other
   ___oppose
   ___strongly oppose

   Why? _____
   _____

4. In choosing a camp for your child, how important would it be that
   the camp have each of the following?

	very important	important	unimportant
children of various religions and ethnic backgrounds	___	___	___
mostly Jewish campers and staff......................	___	___	___
Sabbath services.....................................	___	___	___
classes in Jewish religion...........................	___	___	___
classes in Jewish history and culture...............	___	___	___
kosher food..	___	___	___

5. Do you ever attend lectures or classes of Jewish interest?

   ___yes → About how many sessions like this
            have you attended in the past year?_____
   ___no

6. Do you regularly read any newspapers or magazines of Jewish content?

   ___yes → Which ones? _____
   ___no

Do you regularly read any other newspapers or magazines primarily for their coverage of Israel or other Jewish topics?

   ___yes → Which ones? _____
   ___no

7. On political and social issues, I consider myself a:

   __radical   ___liberal   ___moderate   ___conservative

While I was growing up, my parents considered themselves:

   __radical   ___liberal   ___moderate   ___conservative

8. Which of the following do you remember from your parents' home while you were growing up?

   (check as many as apply)
   ___celebration of Jewish holidays on a regular basis
   ___presence of Jewish magazines or newspapers (in Yiddish or English)
   ___keeping kosher
   ___lighting candles on Friday evening
   ___Jewish ceremonial or art objects
   ___Israeli objects
   ___none of the above

9. Which of the following were regularly discussed in your parents' home while you were growing up?

   (check as many as apply)
   ___Israel
   ___anti-Semitism
   ___synagogue or other local Jewish affairs
   ___labor issues
   ___socialism
   ___none of the above

10. Do you think of yourself as an Orthodox, Conservative, or Reform Jew (not what you belong to, but what you consider yourself)?

    ___Orthodox
    ___Conservative
    ___Reform
    ___Other, specify_____

What did your parents consider themselves while you were growing up?

    ___Orthodox
    ___Conservative
    ___Reform
    ___Other, specify_____

11. Please place an X in the box
which best fits how Jewish   most ←————————→ least
you consider <u>yourself</u>........................ | 5 | 4 | 3 | 2 | 1 | 0 | <u>self</u>

Please place an X in the box
which best fits how Jewish
you consider your <u>spouse</u>.................... | 5 | 4 | 3 | 2 | 1 | 0 | <u>spouse</u>

Please place an X in the box
which best fits how Jewish
you consider <u>your parents</u>.................. | 5 | 4 | 3 | 2 | 1 | 0 | <u>parents</u>

Please place an X in the box
which best fits how Jewish
you <u>would like your children to be</u>.......... | 5 | 4 | 3 | 2 | 1 | 0 | <u>children</u> (hope)

Please place an X in the box
which best fits how Jewish
you <u>think your children will actually be</u>..... | 5 | 4 | 3 | 2 | 1 | 0 | <u>children</u> (expect)

                                              most ←————————→ least

12. How important was each of the following in influencing your current
    level of Jewishness?

	very important	important	not especially important

a. early life experiences:

your Jewish education...........			
your friends while growing up...			
your parental home..............			
other, specify_____			

b. current factors:

your spouse.....................			
your current circle of friends..			
your temple.....................			
your rabbi......................			
Israel..........................			
consciousness of the Holocaust..			
other, specify_____			

13. What is the approximate annual gross income of your household (you and,
    if applicable, your spouse)?

____under $30,000
____$30,000 to $50,000
____$50,000 to $70,000
____$70,000 to $90,000
____over $90,000

14. Do you have any comments about any of the questions you have been asked?

_____

_____

_____

YOU HAVE COMPLETED THE QUESTIONNAIRE.
THANK YOU FOR YOUR TIME AND EFFORT.

PLEASE PLACE THE COMPLETED QUESTIONNAIRE IN THE
STAMPED REPLY ENVELOPE WHICH HAS BEEN PROVIDED
AND DROP IT IN THE MAIL.

Bibliography

De Vos, George. "Ethnic Pluralism: Conflict and Accommodation." In *Ethnic Identity*, edited by George De Vos and Lola Romanucci-Ross. Palo Alto, California: Mayfield Publishing Co., 1975.

Elazar, Daniel J. *Community and Polity: The Organizational Dynamics of American Jewry.* Philadelphia: Jewish Publication Society, 1976.

Ellman, Yisrael. "The Ethnic Awakening in the United States and Its Influence on the Jews." *Ethnicity* 4 (1977):133-155.

Etzioni, Amitai. "The Ghetto-A Reevaluation." *Social Forces* 37 (1959): 255-262.

Fein, Leonard J.; Chin, Robert; Dauber, Jack; Reisman, Bernard; and Spiro, Herzl. *Reform Is A Verb: Notes on Reform and Reforming Jews.* New York: Union of American Hebrew Congregations, 1972.

Fishman, Sylvia Barack. "The Changing American Jewish Family in the 80's." *Contemporary Jewry*, 1987.

Fowler, Floyd J. *1975 Community Survey: A Study of the Jewish Population of Greater Boston.* Boston: Combined Jewish Philanthropies, 1977.

Furman, Frida Kerner. *Beyond Yiddishkeit: The Struggle for Jewish Identity in a Reform Synagogue.* State University of New York Press, 1987.

Gans, Herbert J. "The Origins of a Jewish Community in the Suburbs." In *The Jewish Community in America*, edited by Marshall Sklare. New York: Behrman House, 1974.

_____ . *The Urban Villagers.* New York: Free Press, 1965.

Glazer, Nathan, and Moynihan, Daniel P., eds. *Ethnicity: Theory and Experience.* Cambridge: Harvard University Press, 1975.

Goldscheider, Calvin. *Jewish Continuity and Change.* Bloomington, Indiana: Indiana University Press, 1986.

Goldstein, Sidney. "Jews in the United States: Perspectives from Demography." In *Jewish Life in the United States: Perspectives from the Social Sciences*, edited by Joseph B. Gittler. New York: New York University Press, 1981.

Gordon, Milton. *Assimilation in American Life.* New York: Oxford University Press, 1964.

Greeley, Andrew M. *The Denominational Society.* Glenview, Illinois: Scott, Foresman, 1972.

Guest, Avery M., and Weed, James A. "Ethnic Residential Segregation: Patterns of Change." *American Journal of Sociology* 81 (1976): 1088-1111.

Halpern, Ben. "America Is Different." In *The Jews: Social Patterns of an American Group*, edited by Marshall Sklare. Glencoe, Illinois: Free Press, 1958.

Herberg, Will. *Protestant, Catholic, Jew.* rev. ed. Garden City, New York: Doubleday, Anchor Books, 1960.

_____ . "The Postwar Revival of the Synagogue." *Commentary* 9 (1950): 315-325.

Higham, John. *Send These To Me.* New York: Athenaeum, 1975.

Himmelfarb, Harold. "The Impact of Religious Schooling: The Effects of Jewish Education upon Adult Religious Involvement." Ph.D. dissertation, University of Chicago, 1974.

Hraba, Joseph. *American Ethnicity.* Itasca, Illinois: F.E. Peacock, 1979.

Jick, Leon. *The Americanization of the Synagogue, 1820-1870.* Hanover, New Hampshire: University Press of New England, 1976.

Johnston, Barry V., and Yoels, William C. "On Linking Cultural and Structural Models of Ethnicity: A Synthesis of Schooler and Yancey, Ericksen, and Juliani. *American Journal of Sociology* 83 (1977):729-736.

Kobrin, Frances E., and Goldscheider, Calvin. *The Ethnic Factor in Family Structure and Mobility.* Cambridge, Massachusetts: Ballinger Press, 1978.

Lenn, Theodore I. *Rabbi and Synagogue in Reform Judaism.* New York: Central Conference of American Rabbis, 1972.

Massachusetts Department of Commerce and Development. "City and Town Monographs." Mimeographed. Boston: Massachusetts Department of Commerce and Development.

Massarik, Fred, and Chenkin, Alvin. "United States National Jewish Population Study: A First Report." *American Jewish Year Book* 74 (1973): 264-306.

Nie, Norman H.; Hull, C. Hadlai; Jenkins, Jean G.; Steinbrenner, Karin; and Bent, Dale H. *Statistical Package for the Social Sciences.* 2d.ed. New York: McGraw-Hill, 1975.

Parsons, Talcott. "Some Theoretical Considerations on the Nature and Trends of Change in Ethnicity." In *Ethnicity: Theory and Experience,* edited by Nathan Glazer and Daniel P. Moynihan. Cambridge: Harvard University Press, 1975.

_____ . *The Social System.* Glencoe, Illinois: Free Press, 1951.

Reisman, Bernard. *The Chavurah: A Contemporary Jewish Experience.* New York: Union of American Hebrew Congregations, 1977.

Rosenthal, Erich. "Jewish Intermarriage in Indiana". *American Jewish Year Book* 68 (1967): 243-264.

Schwartz, Barry, ed. *The Changing Face of the Suburbs.* Chicago: University of Chicago Press, 1976.

Silberman, Charles E. *A Certain People.* New York: Summit Books, 1985.

Sklare, Marshall. *America's Jews.* New York: Random House, 1971.

____ . *Conservative Judaism: An American Religious Movement.* Glencoe, Illinois: Free Press, 1955.

Sklare, Marshall, and Greenblum, Joseph. *Jewish Identity on the Suburban Frontier.* New York: Basic Books, 1967.

Treiman, Donald J. *Occupational Prestige in Comparative Perspective.* New York: Academic Press, 1977.

Wirth, Louis. "Ideological Aspects of Social Disorganization." *American Sociological Review* 5 (1940): 472-482.

____ . *The Ghetto.* Chicago: University of Chicago Press, 1928.

Yancey, William L.; Ericksen, Eugene P.; and Juliani, Richard N. "Emergent Ethnicity: A Review and Reformulation." *American Sociological Review* 41 (1978): 391-402.